**Other books by
Paul Semendinger**

Scattering the Ashes

*The Least Among Them: 29 Players, Their Brief Moments in the Big
Leagues, and A Unique History of the New York Yankees*

Roy White: From Compton to the Bronx

365.2

Going The Distance: A Runner's Journey

By

Dr. Paul Semendinger

Artemesia
Publishing

ISBN: 9781951122782 (paperback) / 9781951122799 (ebook)
LCCN: 2023947431

Artemesia Publishing
9 Mockingbird Hill Rd
Tijeras, New Mexico 87059
info@artemesiapublishing.com
www.apbooks.net

DEDICATION

As always, with all my book projects, none of this would be possible without the support of my wife Laurie and my sons, Ryan, Alex, and Ethan. I also wouldn't be the person I am without the love given to me from my parents and my in-laws.

To my many friends who support me in everything, far too many to name, but who especially guided and encouraged me on this quest: Mike, Colin, Ed, Paul, Dan, and so many others—thank you. Thank you, tremendously. Always.

To the wonderful doctors who keep me running—thank you for your dedicated care, your love, your support, and your encouragement.

To the teachers, staff, students, and families of Hawes Elementary School in Ridgewood, New Jersey—thank you for making my years there the most rewarding of my professional career. Each day it was an honor to serve as the principal of that wonderful school. I loved every moment and I love all of you always.

To Sheeraz, you're not here to read this, but thanks for being my friend. Life is far too short. I miss you!

To Geoff, the most wonderful publisher anywhere, thank you for always believing in me. I hope that we have many many more publishing adventures together. I greatly appreciate your support and encouragement!

In everything I do, I give thanks to God for his love and support. I find that He is always with me—especially when I need Him the most. When I walk (or run) through the valley of the shadow of death, God is there. His rod and His staff will always comfort me. I am pleased that God and Jesus are important parts of my life.

Beginning This Story At The End...

What follows is the true account of my successful attempt to run every single day for an entire calendar year.

As such, this is a chronicle of running, but it is also the story of a significant year in my life. It would be impossible to share my running journey without revealing who I am and my life experiences at the time that I completed this quest. As I ran, I also wrote striving to capture the feelings, emotions, and my thoughts in real time.

In keeping with the authenticity of this project, I did not go back and tie up all the loose ends. As part of the writing process, I revised and edited this work countless times, and while I worked to bring a sense of cohesion to the whole project, it is also true that life always moves in new directions—hopefully forward. But, in the end, life isn't always neat and clean. Things do not always work out as we hope or plan. There will always be loose ends that are not tied up at the end of a year... or ever. In keeping this work focused, I also had to leave out many stories, events, and the like. That, too, is in keeping with real life.

2022 was a watershed year for me. New doors opened and a big door closed. Throughout it all, I ran, and ran, and ran.

This account begins on January 1, 2022. I was 53-years-old and working as the principal of the most wonderful elementary school anywhere. This was a job I loved—deeply. I was also an adjunct college professor. A big change in my professional life was coming as, although I had not decided on that decision yet myself, this was the year I would retire as a principal.

I have always been very active. I try to exercise daily. As an athlete, for the most part, I'm nothing special. I never competed athletically in college. I wasn't even good enough to make a varsity sport in high school. But the one thing I do that most people do not, is run marathons. I found that sport in 2002 and it captured me. I continually look for the next marathon to run. I sometimes want to quit running long distances, but I can't.

In addition to running, I still play baseball. There is a large part of me that never wants to grow up.

I have been happily married to my wife Laurie for over thirty years. We're all blessed that my parents and Laurie's parents are all still big parts of our lives. Laurie's brother, Mark, who has special needs, and who is my best friend, also plays a significant role in our lives. We have three wonderful sons: Ryan, Alex, and Ethan. Ryan married his wife Tiffany in 2021. When these people appear in the book, it helps to know who they are.

In certain instances, for confidentiality or for privacy, especially as it related to my professional career, I excluded certain events, or I wrote about some in very vague terms. In some situations, I have changed descriptors to make the individuals or situations discussed unrecognizable to others who might have knowledge of the people or situations I describe. I have also changed the names of some people to respect their privacy, for confidentiality, or otherwise.

As I ran and as I wrote, I realized how very fortunate I am. If there is something notable about me, it is the fact that I seem to have an iron will with great focus and tenacity. I believe in setting goals and working diligently to attain them. I believe in always pushing forward and seeking ways to accomplish new things.

When we strive for greatness, we often find out who we really are.

I believe in success, and I believe in failure.

I often read books and am inspired by the successes, great and small, that others have achieved. It is my hope that this story, this account of my daily running, and my life in 2022, helps to motivate others to set their own goals and to work to live out their own dreams.

We can all do more than we ever thought was possible.

All it takes is taking that very first step...

An Important Note:

THIS IS NOT A BOOK ABOUT RUNNING.

This is the story of a runner (me) as I live through my year of running on a daily basis. Running each day for an entire year was my white whale, one of the things I had to do in my life.

I wrote this book to inspire runners to set their own goals and to work to achieve them. But running is a metaphor. We all have goals, hopes, ambitions, and dreams. Not everyone runs. Not everyone wants to run. Still, we all have dreams. It's my hope that this book helps others to live out their dreams.

This could have just as easily been a book about my attempt to play the piano every day or to read the Bible over the course of a calendar year. This could be the story of a person seeking to read many books or paint his first portrait. Or anything...

People set all sorts of goals. And goals are great. But it's one thing to set a goal and another to find the ways to achieve it. I hope, as I found the ways to achieve this goal, that it can motivate you (the reader) to find ways to achieve yours.

We also don't set goals on a daily basis, but instead we set them over time. There really is no true starting point, nor should there ever be an end to our lifelong quests to achieve.

The Rule of 10,000 basically says that in order to be great at something, a person must spend 10,000 hours at that task. Once a person reaches that mark, he or she could be considered a virtuoso. I've been running for decades, and have covered more than 25,000 miles to date. I figure that's about 5,000 hours of running (probably a bit less). As a runner, I'm about halfway to being a virtuoso.

But, again, it's not about the end. Once I reach 10,000 hours of running, I'll work to reach 10,000 more. Once I accomplish one goal, I set out to do more. It's a lifetime quest to be better in everything I do. And I have a long way to go.

I stumble a lot. I fail a lot. I figure I've spent more than 10,000 hours failing at things. I'm sure I'm a virtuoso at failing.

But, if that's so, I'm also a virtuoso at getting back up and starting again.

That's what I hope the reader gets from this book – the idea that if I can run every day for a year, then you can also certainly do something amazing. You might set out to run every day for two years. Or five. It doesn't matter. At all. I hope everyone surpasses my accomplishment and achieves all they set out to do.

It's all about always moving forward. One day at a time.

JANUARY

"Bid me run, and I will strive with things impossible."
William Shakespeare, *Julius Caesar*

Saturday, January 1, 2022
  Day 1 – 5.1 miles

As I begin this significant journey and somewhat ridiculous quest, I look forward to the challenge of daily running with both anticipation and dread. I want to do this. More, I *need* to do this. Running every day for a year has been a compulsion of mine for at least a decade, probably longer. I often think of things I wish to accomplish. Some are big things and some small – some meaningless and others important. There is something essential in life about setting goals, no matter how meaningless they might seem at first. I have often wondered if I could run every single day for an entire year. I also don't think this is meaningless. This is something I think I need to do.

And to do it there's only one starting point. Today. The first day of the year.

I am somewhat afraid to begin. I know this will be very difficult. I know there will be days when I dread running. I have a pretty strong feeling that I'll hurt myself. I don't want that. I also know that once I get too far into this, I will not be able to stop. This could become all-consuming. I'm not looking forward to any of that. But I have to give this a try. If I don't, I will think about this all year and resolve on the first day next year to undertake this challenge. If I don't begin today, I will be feeling these same emotions at this time next year. The only difference is that another year will have passed, and I will be that much older. I'm getting to the point where I am not sure how many years I have left where I can consider doing something like this. I'm approaching my mid-fifties when most people slow down. The clock is ticking. In many ways, for me, it's now... or never.

The fact that I have not attained this life goal frustrates me because I am tired of thinking about this challenge, starting this task, and not following through by being unable to complete it. In this regard, I'm tired of feeling like a failure. If I set a goal for myself and I fail to attain that goal, to me, that's failure. I don't like to fail. I know that running every single day will be difficult for many reasons. But in a different sense it's also very difficult to keep putting off a goal. On January 1 next year I want to look back knowing that I faced a monumental physical challenge and succeeded in overcoming it.

I will never forgive myself if I don't complete this task. One of these years I'm going to run every single day. It might as well be this year.

I am excited to begin. I am also overwhelmed with the thought of the task ahead of me. I am fearful, but I am full of anticipation.

Life is made up of contradictions.

***

They say the third time is the charm. I hope it is. I have attempted this task twice before and failed both times. I don't like to fail. When I fall short of my goals, when I quit, I see weakness in myself. I would like to think that I am stronger than any and all of the circumstances that surround me. But that's not always true.

The first time I tried to run every day for an entire year was in 2017. It didn't go well. I made it to January 4. Big deal. After running for just three days that year, I had had enough. I couldn't sustain the motivation needed to run every day. I think, deep down, I was afraid of committing too much to the ordeal that was to come. I stopped because I was afraid. I quit on myself. I failed.

The next time I tried was the very next year. I did better that time. I made it to February 23 for a total of 53 consecutive days of running.

That was no small feat. But, to be honest, I hated it. My heart wasn't totally in it. Rather than being something great, it was one more thing I had to do. I tried to find the easy way out far too often by running as little as possible. I was getting there, but it wasn't authentic and because of that, I ultimately failed.

This year is different. I am tired of thinking about doing this. I need to get it done. This time I have the focus and the correct frame of mind. I am mentally and physically ready for this challenge.

I appreciate running more today than I did even a few years ago. In 2017 and 2018, my body was slowly breaking down. I had an assortment of injuries, many that runners typically face at one time or another, but as I was getting older, into my fifties, the injuries weren't getting better. I had one particular injury, one that I kept running through, that was a ticking time bomb. I had tears in my right Achilles tendon. Each time I ran, I made the tears worse. I gutted through the pain for years, but it eventually got in the way of me being able to be the athlete and the runner I need to be. I finally had surgery in January 2020 to repair my Achilles tendon.

Once I could finally run again, after shedding the crutches, the walking boot, and after going through months of painful physical therapy, I resolved to appreciate the sport of running more. The months of not being able to run helped me to develop a new appreciation for this activity.

I also learned how difficult it is to start anew. I knew it would take time, perseverance, and a great deal of patience to become a runner again. I also still wanted to be able to run marathons. I knew there would be pain. Running hurts. It just does. And when one starts running, it hurts even more. Running is difficult. It is often not fun. As I started running, I learned again why people hate this sport. But I was determined to find a way to love running once again.

I'm getting older. But I'm also too young to quit being vigorous. When I am active, I feel more alive.

***

To kick off my year of running, I had considered taking part in a local race, the First Day 5K in Fair Lawn, New Jersey, but it was raining, so I decided to go to my steady and loyal stand-by, my treadmill. I run a lot on my treadmill.

I wanted to begin 2022 with a good solid run. My goal was to reach five miles. I set a simple formula:

Mile 1 at 6.0 miles per hour.
Mile 2 at 6.1 miles per hour.
Mile 3 at 6.2 mph
Mile 4 at 6.3 mph and
Mile 5 at 6.4 mph

It was a struggle, but I did it. Big tasks are often easier when they are broken down into smaller segments.

I usually do a little "cool down" after the run is completed. Most often this adds an extra tenth of a mile to my total miles covered for the day. While I ran five miles, with the cool down, I actually covered 5.10 miles.

I have one day down. There are 364 to go.

Sunday, January 2, 2022
   Day 2 – 2.1 miles

One of the first things I needed to determine as I embarked on this journey was to decide what actually counts as a day of running. To answer this, I researched "streakers" (that's what they're called— people who run every day) and the common answer seems to be just one mile. That simple fact makes this long unrelenting goal seem a little bit more attainable. I think I can run one mile a day. One little mile seems reasonable.

(Is reasonable even a fair adjective for running every day for a calendar year?)

***

I usually run first thing in the morning, but I wasn't able to get to my run today until 8:30 p.m.

I began today by walking with a friend, Mike. We have been walking together for years and have a three-mile route that we cover together once each week. I enjoy our weekly walks, but they don't count as runs. Walking isn't running. So, while we covered some miles, I still had to find the time to run.

After the walk, Ethan and I went to the Jets game to watch Ethan's favorite football player, the great Tom Brady. This might be Brady's last year in the NFL, and this was the only time his team, the Tampa Bay Buccaneers, would be in town.

It was a fantastic game. In the end, Tom Brady marched his team 90 yards in the final two minutes to secure the victory. Last season Tom Brady led his team to a Super Bowl victory. It was the seventh time he's been a Super Bowl winning quarterback. He might just do it again this year. There are rumors that if he wins it all again, that he will retire. I always like to see great players go out on top. In my professional life, that's what I plan to do. I also want to go out on top.

When we returned home, I didn't have the ability to immediately run. All day long, even at the game, I was answering e-mails and texts on my phone.

We will be returning to school, full time, tomorrow for the first time since we shut down for Covid in 2020. We're returning just as Covid cases are spiking. As a principal, I pride myself on being available for the parents at all times. I can't think of a better way to demonstrate my commitment and my dedication to the school and the community. Many people think I'm crazy, but I give my phone number to the parents each year at Back-to-School Night. I tell them, "If you need me, I'm available."

When we love what we do, we give it everything we have. This is how I run my school and how I live my life. I try not to take shortcuts. If it is worth doing, it's worth doing well.

Because this is all so unprecedented, returning to fulltime school, establishing new procedures and safeguards, and so much more, in the midst of a pandemic, there are a lot of questions being asked by everyone: the district leaders, the school principals, the teachers, the parents, and the community. There is a lot of fear right now. Last night the elementary principals in my district (there are six of us) had a virtual meeting to establish some parameters for the return to school tomorrow. We have discussed all of this for weeks, but things are always changing.

This is now the third consecutive school year impacted by Covid, and still so much is new, uncertain, and (quite frankly) unknown. Much of the time, we are dealing with questions that no one knows the answers to. Many of the questions don't even have any answers. That's what makes so much of this so challenging. The rules change. The approaches change.

The other principals and I make a great team, but we don't agree on everything. We all bring different strengths to our schools, and we run our schools very differently. It becomes extremely challenging to find approaches that work for all our schools as we address situations we never before had to solve. We care deeply about what we do, and we are doing everything we can to keep everyone safe, and to have schools where learning takes place, and students are cared for in a time of angst, worry, and great confusion.

***

It's only the second day of the year, but, after such a long day, I thought about taking the easy way out and only running one mile on my treadmill. "I just need to keep the streak alive today," I rationalized. But as I ran, I felt good, and pushed to reach two miles knowing that in less than 12 hours I'll be running again.

Monday, January 3, 2022
Day 3 – 3.1 miles

On most workdays, I get up at about 4:00 a.m. as I did today.

Some people linger in bed when the alarm clock rings. I don't. I usually wake naturally before the alarm, but if it does ring, I quickly turn it off and immediately get going. I can't lie in bed waiting for the day to catch me. I always need to be ahead of the day. This is who I am. I began waking up super early during my doctoral work. I wanted to be available to be a daddy and husband. The only time when I could work without taking away from my family was when they were all sleeping. This approach became my habit. I am motivated to succeed in all I do, even more, I am determined to succeed. I can only get there by getting up and getting started.

I begin my days by checking my e-mail. Today I received the following message:

> *Happy New Year! Just wanted to reach out and let you know that after a lot of consideration, we have decided to keep our daughter home this week. With a young baby at home, we're trying the best we can to manage our risk and want to keep her home until the new covid case metric starts to normalize. We will reassess at the end of the week. I'm sure balancing all of this as an educator is very difficult, but if there is any way we can help her keep up with her school work this week, please let us know.*

This is a perfect an example of what we're facing in schools right now. The fear and trepidation are real. Parents are scared. Teachers are scared. This has to have an impact, and not a positive one, on our students.

It can't be good for kids to grow up in a world of frightened adults.

When I grew up, the adults all seemed fearless. That gave me great comfort because as a child I was scared of a lot.

***

This morning, I banged out a fast three-miles on the treadmill. If I can run at under 9-minute-mile pace, that's fast for me. I wanted to run further, but I know I have to run again tomorrow and since I just started this whole every day running thing, I'm trying to be somewhat smart about all of this. I don't want to overdo a run and burn myself out, or, worse yet, get injured.

After the run, as I do on most mornings, I soaked for a few minutes in my hot tub outside. I do this as often as I can. This time alone outside is where I can find some true peace and solace. I sometimes use this time to pray, but today I simply sat in the hot bubbling water and relaxed.

Tuesday, January 4, 2022
Day 4 – 4.1 miles

I wanted to run a little longer today, but I didn't have the energy or the focus (and both are essential) to having a successful run. There are times when I cut a run short because I don't have the stamina, but just as often, if I stop short of my goal, it is because I cannot maintain the focus needed to keep going.

My mind is always racing, thinking of all the things I am responsible for. I often use my runs as a distraction from everything else, but sometimes I can't put my work out of my mind, and as a result, the run becomes something that gets in the way. Once that happens, once the stresses of my job enter into mind, my run is doomed.

This is one reason I wake up so early each morning. It is the only way for me to make the time needed for exercise while still being able to accomplish everything else I need to do.

I feel proud of myself when I run long distances. The long run indicates to me that I am strong and vibrant. These are feelings I crave and ones that keep me going. Unfortunately, these feelings never last very long, and I feel the need to challenge myself daily.

***

One of my biggest fans called me yesterday to request an autographed copy of *The Least Among Them*, my book that provides a very unique history of the New York Yankees. She wanted a signed copy to give to a friend. I dropped off the book on my way to work.

That big fan is my mom.

***

The return to school yesterday went very well. The kids and the teachers all seemed happy and relieved to be back and at school in person. No one wants to go back to on-line learning. And there is this overarching fear that the schools may be closed again at any moment. I get asked about this multiple times each day. "Do you think we'll be closing?" For now, the answer is no.

I am fearful that our schools could be closed, and not necessarily because of sickness, but because we might run out of teachers who can report to work. Yesterday we had numerous teachers out not because they were sick, but because of the rules regarding close contacts. It looks like tomorrow we will have more teachers out.

I spent my morning plugging holes and finding unique ways to run the school in the absence of so many teachers. Part of the problem is that we do not have enough substitute teachers. Most of our substitute teachers are older people, and many older people are not willing to come into the schools right now. This could become unsustainable in a hurry.

One local school had 17 teachers out today. That is my fear. How do you run a school with no teachers?

My school had only three teachers out. For whatever reason my school seems, continually, to have the lowest number of Covid cases in the district and the best teacher attendance.

Whatever we are all doing in my school, we seem to be doing it right.

Or we've just been very lucky.

Wednesday, January 5, 2022
Day 5 – 3.1 miles

Before I go any further, I need to introduce a key supporting ac-

tor in this journey—my NordicTrack Elite 9700 Pro treadmill, or as I call it, "the TM." A great deal of my running takes place on the TM. I have had this model since September 2011. I have run thousands of miles on this machine.

If I get injured this year, my quest to run each day will come to an end. If the TM breaks, the same could possibly happen.

I run on the treadmill when it's too cold outside. I use it when it's snowing or raining. I sometimes run inside when it's too hot. I most often run in the early morning when it's still dark outside and that's a big reason why I'm on the TM so often.

I don't like running outside in the dark. There are far too many dangers outside in the early morning: cars, delivery trucks, dogs, racoons, skunks, potholes, sticks... any number of things. In the winter, ice is always an issue.

I'm not afraid of the dark, but when it comes to running outside before daylight, I am a little afraid. I much prefer running where it is safe—at home on the TM.

Thursday, January 6, 2022
  Day 6 – 4.1 miles

This morning's run was tedious. I usually vary my pace to generate some interest and variety in what I'm doing, but today I stayed at 6.0 MPH and just ran, albeit a little slower than I would have preferred.

I am trying to pace myself a bit, not quite knowing, yet, how to conceptualize what it is to run every single day for an entire year. Because of this, I am trying to make smart decisions such as how I handled today's run. On days like today, I am simply trying to get the run in. I'm not trying to run fast. I'm just striving to run.

***

Thus far, even as the school deals with teacher shortages, we're making it work. The teachers, when necessary, are covering for each other—and even for the principal.

Yesterday there was so much ice on the roads that I couldn't make it to work on time. For whatever reason, our town wasn't prepared for the ice. They never put salt or anything down and the roads were far too slick. That's never happened to me before. Cars were sliding everywhere. My commute is only six miles, but much of it is down-hill. Yesterday, in just the first few minutes of driving, I realized that there was no way I could manage the hills safely. I turned around and went back home until the roads got better.

In my absence, or, more accurately, in my delay in getting to work, the teachers and the secretaries did all the things I would have. They covered for me. That's the mark of a special school.

Friday, January 7, 2022
Day 7 – 3.1 miles

We actually have a snow day today. The snow was coming down heavy overnight. In our area, snow days are called when it seems the snow will be deep enough (a few inches at least) or the roads bad enough (yesterday was a huge exception) to make driving haz-ardous. This decision is made by the superintendent of each school district so there are times when one town has school and the town right next door does not. It's an interesting dynamic to say the least. For whatever reason, days like today seem like a bonus—a special gift. These are free days, in a sense, to do whatever we wish.

Of course, I'll spend a lot of time clearing my driveway and then my in-laws' driveway of the snow.

I only reached three miles today. I'm already getting tired of running on the treadmill day after day. I wanted to run further, but I again did not have the focus to keep going. I'm a little down about this because before I started running today, I was sure I had a little more in me.

I should probably take solace in the fact that I have now run every day for an entire week. But then again, I have 51 more weeks to go.

Saturday, January 8, 2022
Day 8 – 3.1 miles

Today another great friend, Colin, joined Mike and me on our walk. Our sons were all in Boy Scouts together and we all served as leaders in various capacities. Good people bring out the best in me and these are two of the best people I know.

One of the best school leaders I ever worked for was the principal of Pompton Lakes High School when I was just beginning my career as an administrator. I learned a great deal from him. He taught me to always hire people better than myself. He shared that effective leaders bring in people who challenge them. It is through challenges that good leaders become great.

At some point, we all want to be told how great we are, but I have found that the strongest leaders value opposing viewpoints. I have worked for some excellent leaders who value deep thought, reason, and open dialogue. These people brought out the best in me.

I have also worked for some leaders who were less than effective and who hated to be challenged. I once worked for a boss who threatened to give me a written reprimand because in a private conversation with that person, I offered a vision different than what that leader was proposing. In other words, I was told, "Don't disagree with me."

The teachers who have made me a better principal have been the ones who tell me where I need to improve. It's not fun to be told where our weaknesses lie, but open dialogue makes me a more effective leader.

Being open to honest critique is not easy. There was a time when I would get frustrated and sometimes angry when hearing honest and fair criticism. I wasn't as strong of a leader back then. I wish I had truly understood and embraced all of this earlier in my career. I would be better for it.

***

Today is a big anniversary for me. It was two years ago today, that I had the surgery on my right Achilles tendon.

I remember going in for the surgery knowing that weeks of crutches and months of physical therapy lay before me. I checked in at the reception desk at the surgery center and said, "I'm here to register for the 2020 New York City Marathon." The receptionist just smiled and said, "You must be Paul."

This morning I sent a text to the wonderful orthopedist who repaired my Achilles, thanking him for his great work. He texted me back saying, "*Paul, it's you who is an inspiration!*"

***

One fictional character has always been an inspiration to me—Rocky Balboa. I have watched the Rocky movies more times than I can count. I know many of the movies by heart, line-by-line. I always found the character Rocky Balboa to be an inspiration. I appreciate how he was a loser of sorts but through hard work, strong character, and rock-solid determination he overcame all the things in life that seemed against him. Most of all, I love his heart. He would simply never give up. He was a great fighter, a good person, and, if one looks closely enough, a religious fellow as well. There was a time I thought I'd like to be a fighter, just like Rocky, but I'm sure I wouldn't be good at taking punches.

Like Rocky, I just want to go the distance.

Throughout the movie series, Rocky always finds a way to succeed. Through my life, I have also succeeded a great deal. I have a great family. I have a great job. I've earned advanced degrees, I'm a leader. I've run a ton of marathons. I still play baseball. I have written books and had them published. In many ways I've attained many of my life's goals.

I have been wondering though, if I still have that drive in me. Most of the goals I set for myself I accomplished years ago. I wonder if I can still set a high goal, a super unrealistic goal, and achieve it. I'm at the age when most people slow down. I sometimes wonder if my best days are behind me...

One day I'd like to meet Sylvester Stallone. More, as crazy as this sounds, I'd like to meet Rocky Balboa, even though I know that's not really possible.

My son Ryan had an extra TV that he recently gave us. It's gigantic. I put it in the exercise room with the TM, swapping out my older (and much smaller) set. This new TV can be connected to the internet and I started fooling with the controls. I found a montage of work-outs from the Rocky movies on YouTube. The video was 23:53 in length. I wondered if I could run three miles before the video ended.

I finished the run in 23:46.

Sunday, January 9, 2022
    Day 9 – 2.1 miles

I'm struggling right now with a few extra pounds that won't go away. One culprit is that I love soda. I have a ton of it in my office right now and at least once a day, I crack open a Coke.

The fact that I love cola also contributes to the battle I have with high blood sugar. I'm not diabetic, but I am concerned that one day I will be. For years, I tested my glucose when I woke up in the morning, but my physician stopped the prescription that allowed for the testing strips. I'm not quite sure why he cancelled this because it was working to keep my blood sugar levels low.

***

Speaking of sweetness, I need to mention the one person who makes all my dreams possible, my wonderful wife Laurie.

We began dating in high school, in eleventh grade, way back in 1984.

Laurie is the love of my life. She is my constant support. She takes care of so much in our lives which allows me the time to be a principal, to write books, to run a Yankees website, to do podcasts, and to run and exercise incessantly... and more. We're a great team. We understand each other completely.

Without Laurie, this quest wouldn't be possible. But, more importantly, without Laurie, I wouldn't be possible.

***

I had an easy run today. I did just two miles and purposefully ran slowly because I had run so fast yesterday.

I also did some pitching in my basement. I have been pitching in two men's baseball leagues for the last few years. One team plays on Sunday mornings, the other team on a weekday night. A few years ago, the boys gave me a big net to throw baseballs into. I have developed a routine that I follow to help me get into "pitching shape" for the upcoming baseball

season. Most people stop playing baseball long before they get to my age, but I'm preparing for my best season yet.

Monday, January 10, 2022
Day 10 – 5.1 miles

Last week at school went much better than anyone could have anticipated. By the time this is published, some people might forget that as we all came back from lockdowns, the schools required everyone to wear masks. It was a strange dynamic to be in a school and not be able to see the children's faces.

We've been doing well with the return so far, but today might prove to be the most difficult day yet. A few teachers alerted me over the weekend that they have tested positive for Covid. They'll be out all week. We do not have any substitutes who picked up these assignments.

Because of this, I woke up at 3:20 a.m. and couldn't get back to sleep. The concerns of running the school effectively without the necessary personnel is troublesome. We used to have a larger staff of strong and effective teaching assistants who we could use to help fill empty positions in the absence of substitutes, but these positions have been cut drastically the last few years. We went from over 20 teaching assistants just a few years ago, to under 10 this year.

Of course, the people who made those decisions to cut staff so drastically rarely come into the schools themselves to see the results of their decision making. This is one of the aspects of how school districts operate that frustrates me greatly.

***

Because of the snow day, I had not shaved since last Thursday. This used to be a good look for me as it gave me a certain rugged demeanor. Today I looked at my beard and it was full of grey. I didn't look tough, at all. I just looked old. When I'm worn down, I see my grandfather in my reflection in the mirror more than myself. That's never encouraging.

Since I was up early, I had the chance to push my running distance a little. I didn't run fast, but I reached five miles equaling my longest run of the year. This feels like an accomplishment.

I consider myself an average runner. I'm not particularly fast. I don't have the greatest form. But the one thing I can do is run marathons, races of 26.2 miles.

The New York City Marathon is run on the first Sunday of November each year. I usually complete a 16-week training period to prepare for the marathon. The training period begins in July, but this year, since I am running every day, the entire year will be a build-up to the big race. I consider five miles a solid base to build my marathon training upon.

Tuesday, January 11, 2022
  Day 11 – 5.1 miles

At the tail end of last week, I was fighting the slightest of colds. I had the slightest "tickle" in my throat and a very dry occasional cough. This happens to me every year when the weather is very cold as it has been. I don't get sick very often, which I attribute, at least in part, to the fact that I lead a vigorous life. I believe that exercising makes my body and its ability to fight off the common cold stronger.

If I get sick, or come down with Covid, this streak will end. I certainly don't want that. I also won't be able to go to work—and that would be a disaster. I need to be at my school.

Sometimes, when I feel an illness coming on, I wear extra layers of clothing when I run to try to sweat the sickness out of my system. None of this is actual science or medicine, of course, but, for me, it seems to work.

***

I did five miles again today. I pushed it, hard. I love how strenuous activity makes me feel. As I push myself, in spite of being physically tired, I somehow feel stronger.

I believe that exercise invigorates the body. The feeling I had as I ran today is one that I wish I could capture every day when I run.

***

This afternoon I will start my newest book project. I will be working with former Yankees great Roy White on his autobiography. This will be my first collaboration with a former Major League Baseball player. It's a dream come true!

We have a Google Meet set-up for 4:00 p.m.

I can't wait!

Wednesday, January 12, 2022
   Day 12 – 3.1 miles

"I can't wait." What a trite and silly phrase.

We often have to wait. Sometimes the best things in life are worth waiting for. If we can't wait for something, what do we do? Explode?

I have to wait a little longer for my first session with Roy White. He had to reschedule. We'll try again on Friday. (I can't wait!)

***

After two five-mile days, I decided a solid three-miler would be appropriate. I put the TM at 6.0 MPH and like a metronome ran at the same pace for thirty minutes. I don't enjoy runs like this as much because they are very tedious, but when I finish, I am very proud of myself for maintaining the focus and having the perseverance to get through it.

This is one of the keys to completing any task—eventually the task, no matter how boring or miserable, ends. I think of thoughts like this on long runs and especially during marathons. I know that in a short time the task will be over. One of my favorite motivational sayings is, "Pain is temporary, pride is forever." I am thinking of that a lot as I run each day. This has just started, and it hasn't all been fun, but I know that when I complete this year of running, I'll be able to always look back with satisfaction at having accomplished this goal that has consumed me for so long.

***

How does an author know he's "arrived"? One way might be when he sees his book for sale in a Barnes and Noble store, as I did today.

As I perused the sports books, I saw *The Least Among Them* on the shelf. I took the book, my book, in my hands, quickly autographed it, and put it back on the shelf. I felt both a little famous and a little like I did something wrong.

Thursday, January 13, 2022
Day 13 – 3.1 miles

My run today was a drag. I didn't want to run. I had no interest nor motivation. I considered running later in the day, after work, thinking that I might be more motivated then, but I have this fear that if I put off a run, the day might escape me. As such, I got ready and jumped on the TM.

I hated every single step of the three miles I covered on the treadmill.

I didn't consider that all this running might make me hate something that is a major part of my life.

***

As a runner, I maintain a detailed running log. This is one way I hold myself accountable. My records date back to the late 1990s. I keep track of my daily, weekly, and monthly mileage along

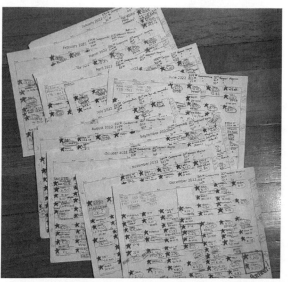

with my fastest runs. I like to know how fast I am (or was). I'm always looking for ways to improve. By keeping track of my runs, I can measure my performance against myself. I'm not as fast as I was a decade or two decades ago, but I can still see how I did compared with the day before, the week before, the month before, and even the years before. All of this information helps to drive me—it gives me cold hard statistics for goals to try to reach, such as my longest or fastest run over any period of time.

Sometimes I still think that I just might have my fastest runs still lurking somewhere deep inside me.

Friday, January 14, 2022
   Day 14 – 6.1 miles

A somewhat noteworthy Hollywood director reached out to me a few months ago with a sincere interest in adapting my novel, *Scattering the Ashes*, into a movie. I have always been a big dreamer and have been waiting, eagerly and with great hope, for the call where he confirms his interest.

Today, I finally got a response in an e-mail, and it wasn't what I was hoping for:

   Hi Paul

   I hope you had a nice holiday. I had a chance to read Ashes and it is a sweet story. Congrats on writing it and getting it published!

   Unfortunately, I am looking for a much edgier story to adapt.

   Sorry I didn't have better news.

   Warmly,
   (The Director)

To say I am disappointed is an understatement. I know that my book will one day make an outstanding movie.

Before it was published, *Scattering the Ashes* faced many rejections, because, as I was told over and over, it was too nice of a story. Numerous literary agents felt it needed to be edgier. I disagree, vehemently. There is still, and there always will be, a place for books that are uplifting.

I have a still unpublished picture book about a father and a son who spend a day in New York's Central Park together. It's a great story filled with images of imagination. The story is one that celebrates a special day in the life of a child, simply spending the day with his dad. I have been told that the story needs some conflict between the father and the son in order to be publishable.

I have to wonder, isn't the world edgy enough?

***

Today I wasn't able to run before work. I had too much to do. There are mornings when I wake up and am inundated with messages, questions, and other concerns. As much as I need to run, the responsibilities of my job are always more important. I was very pleased that when I ran after work, I was able to push the distance and cover six miles.

I am 14-for-14. Two full weeks of running are now completed. After days like this, I am full of confidence, energy, anticipation, and hope.

And I feel very strong.

Saturday, January 15, 2022
   Day 15 – 3.1 miles

There is something special about getting a new pair of running shoes. Most runners have their favorite shoe brands and styles. I run in the Brooks Adrenaline. I ordered a new pair online the other day, and they just arrived.

These new running shoes have a USA type design. I usually wear dark colored shoes, but these are white with red and blue highlights—almost flag like. They're fun. Ryan has the same shoes. Since my previous running shoes went over 400 miles, it was time for a change. As runners, we need to keep track of how many miles we run in our shoes. If one runs too many miles in the same running shoe, he has a higher chance of sustaining an injury. I'm not much into fashion. I don't often purchase new clothes. In fact, I don't like

shopping at all. Still, I like getting new sneakers. There is something special about a brand new pair.

***

As a principal, I wear a suit and tie to work each day. I believe it is important to dress as a leader. But, because I'm with children, my ties have cartoon characters on them—most often with images of Disney or Charlie Brown characters. I have hundreds of ties accumulated over a long career.

I wear sneakers with my suits rather than dress shoes. I started this after the 2018 New York City Marathon after running that race with a stress fracture in my foot. I'm on my feet most of the day and sneakers just feel better.

It's an original look, but it's me. One of the great facets of my school is that the community accepts me as I am. We talk a lot about unconditional love. I try to always give unconditional love to everyone. I am certain it comes back to me in greater amounts than I ever gave.

Sunday, January 16, 2022
   Day 16 – 5.1 miles

I woke up today thinking, "Fifteen days down, 350 to go. Piece of cake."

If only.

***

One of these days I'll get outside to run, but it's just about zero degrees today.

Most often on the treadmill, I invent a pattern to follow for my run. Today I did an exercise I call "Semmer 400's." In short, each quarter-mile, I increase the speed slightly, until a mile is completed. At that point, I slow down, but to a faster starting pace than the mile I just finished. Today's run followed the following pattern (with each number meaning miles-per-hour):

Mile 1: 6.0, 6.1, 6.2, 6.3
Mile 2: 6.1, 6.2, 6.3, 6.4
Mile 3: 6.2, 6.3, 6.4, 6.5
Mile 4: 6.3, 6.4, 6.5, 6.6
Mile 5: 6.4, 6.5, 6.6, 6.7

A run like this produces "negative splits" meaning each mile is run slightly faster than the mile before it. I believe exercises like this help me become a stronger runner.

I am often thinking about my next marathon. My goal is to continually get stronger so that the final miles of the race don't crush me. (In truth, I often have to walk a bit in the last miles of a marathon. As I get older, I find that I am not always strong enough to gut through the high miles without walking breaks.)

***

Roy White and I began our work on his autobiography. We talked for over an hour focusing on his life growing up as a kid in Compton. It was great. I loved every second. I haven't had many opportunities to talk to former Major League baseball players. I hope this is the start of a positive collaboration together.

Monday, January 17, 2022
Day 17 – 3.1 miles

My calves were very sore yesterday. One of my biggest concerns about my ability to run every day is that I am not allowing my body enough time to rest and recover from one day to the next.

I wonder if I should run very late one night and very early the next morning to build in some extra consecutive hours of rest. I'm thinking of a run just before midnight and then another just after. That could work.

***

At school we're off today for Rev. Dr. Martin Luther King, Jr.'s birthday.

I look forward to the day when no one looks at race or ethnicity or any physical characteristic and uses those as ways to define someone else.

We're all God's people. The sooner we all realize that, the better we all will be.

Tuesday, January 18, 2022
Day 18 – 5.1 miles

Before the injury to my Achilles, I never used to do stretching or any loosening up before I ran. The research on the benefits of stretching is somewhat conflicting, and since, years ago, I never seemed to get badly injured, I just ignored that whole process. Stretching takes time, something I don't have a lot of. I didn't want to waste time doing something that I didn't think would be of any value.

That's no longer the case. Stretching is now part of my pre-run routine. My physical therapists taught me some stretches that I now follow religiously. Ethan also taught me a warm-up routine that I also follow before every run. I am hoping these exercises help to prevent any future injuries or set-backs. They're working so far!

Today, I ran five miles doing Semmer 400's a little faster than the other day. I really pushed myself and was absolutely exhausted as I finished. At the same time, because I gave so much of myself, I was also full of energy and enthusiasm.

This is what I live for – pushing myself as hard as I can. Challenging workouts make me feel more alive.

A few years ago, I started playing baseball, not softball, but real baseball. I am a pitcher. At my age, no one expects me to be able to throw a full nine-inning game, but I do that often enough. I enjoy digging deep and finding something inside myself to succeed.

I ran today with a few layers of clothes on, including long sleeve running shirts and a sweatshirt. I did this so I will sweat more and hopefully lose some weight. One might think that with all this running, I'd be losing weight, but the running is giving me an excuse to eat more – and when I eat, more often than not, I'm consuming junk food. I am stuck in a bad pattern.

Twice this year when I've run really hard while wearing layers, like I did today, I find that after the run, I urinate blood. This has happened to me a number of times over the years when I have exerted myself really hard and for longer distances, usually without proper hydration.

The blood doesn't scare me as much as it did when this first started first happening years ago. I have found that it's the natural result of not drinking enough. It eventually goes away, but it is never a pleasant thing. Sometimes I make the mistake of not drinking when I run. I don't know why I do this—deep down I think it's to replicate how I might feel in a long run with no opportunities for a drink of water or Gatorade, but it makes very little sense, and it is a very bad practice.

Wednesday, January 19, 2022
   Day 19 – 6.1 miles

Sometimes when one runs, he just finds a flow. I found that flow today. I knew, almost from the very start, that I had six miles in me.

There are times when I run when I know I'll reach my goals for the day. There's just a sense, a confidence, a knowing, that it will happen. Other times, I am riddled with doubt. This has nothing to do with conditioning. It's a strange dynamic. The human body and mind sometimes work extremely well together. Other times, they don't.

I found that flow today. I wish there was a way to find that flow every day.

***

About a decade ago, I ran a local 5K race and was especially fast. I was so proud of myself. I found a groove and ran hard the entire way. I was flying! My legs were strong and my mind was too.

After the race, I couldn't wait to see the race photos. I wanted to see how great I looked. I wanted to see me at my best.

Usually when the race photos are posted on-line, they are categorized by the runner's race number. That didn't occur for this race. Instead, they posted the photos in the order the photographer took them. Knowing my race time, I figured I'd find my photos quickly enough.

I remember going through them, one at a time:

"I remember that kid."
"I saw that guy."
"I passed him."
"I couldn't catch her..."

I quickly scanned photo after photo, yet I couldn't find myself:

"High school kid."
"Yellow Shirt guy."
"Old man."
"Very fit woman."
"Pony tail."
"Bright shoes…"

I went through the photos again and again, making the same observations time after time.

"Yellow shirt guy."
"Old man."
"Very fit woman."
"Pony tail…"

I knew that I finished right with those runners. I remembered them all.

Except the old man.

It turns out that the old man was me.

I didn't buy the race photo.

Thursday, January 20, 2022
    Day 20 – 3.1 miles

More snow and today we have a delayed opening. That's two hours less of school, but much of that time will be shoveling my driveway, then doing the same at my in-laws, and then maybe even doing some snow removal at school. Yes, I'm a principal who also helps shovel the snow.

When I run on my treadmill at home, I listen to music on my iPod. I've been listening to the same songs for many years, but they suit me well. A lot of the songs are motivational. Many come from the Rocky movies. If I'm running especially hard, I often listen to loud rock or songs with very positive messages. One day I'll make a list of my top ten favorite running songs. The only problem is that the list often changes!

Sometimes I sing when I run. Unfortunately, I don't sing particularly well. When I'm finished with a run and the rest of the family is behind closed doors, I know that my singing was particularly obnoxious that day.

***

Tonight is Bingo Night for my school. I'll call Bingo, but like so many events these last years, I'll be doing this from home via Zoom. It's Virtual Bingo. We used to do this event live, in person, with people gathered at tables around the gym, but we're still immersed in Covid rules. It will be fine this way, but it's not the same. I miss seeing people in person.

Social events lose something when they are not... social.

Friday, January 21, 2022
Day 21 – 3.25 miles

28 years ago today, my oldest son Ryan was born. We'll drive out to Pennsylvania tomorrow to see Ryan and his wife Tiffany at their home in Hershey. I look forward to running with Ryan. I haven't had a running buddy yet this year. It'll be wonderful to run with my son.

As far as running today, I didn't have it. At all.

I thought I might go six or seven miles, but I pushed through a somewhat fast three miles and stopped. I breathed deeply thinking I had a few more miles in me. All I had to do was start the treadmill again. It would have taken but one second of effort to get the machine going. But I couldn't do it. I was completely done.

21 consecutive days of running, all on the treadmill, even for me, is getting tedious. But, worse than that, I feel I failed myself. I need to be able to find the mental strength, the singularity of purpose, to overcome any discomfort, pain, boredom, or lack of focus and push

beyond the minimum. This is how success comes. Today, by quitting, I tasted only failure. This is a feeling I don't enjoy. At all.

***

A grandparent of a first-grade student at my school shared the following story with me:

The family was playing a board game and a question was posed to the little girl, "Would you rather live in the past or the future?"
The child replied, "The past. I'd like to live before there was ever Covid."

That story took me aback. Most kids, most often, think about the future. Kids like to say things like, "When I grow up…" Children dream forward. I think we all do. But this child wishes for the past. She is six years old. She's never been in school without seeing people with their faces covered by masks. For her entire life outside of her home, she has been told to keep her distance from others. She longs for something different, and even as a child, she knows that things are not normal.

Children naturally touch other kids. They hug, tag, and tackle each other. It's part of natural play and has been forever. We now have children who have never done any of those things. We have children who are forbidden from doing the things that kids have always done.

Then, yesterday, a second grader showed me a toy he had. Kids do this a lot. I reached out to pick it up and another child said, "Don't play with that, you might spread Covid-19."

Those were his exact words.

And he was deadly serious.

Saturday, January 22, 2022
    Day 22 – 3.05 miles

22 for 22 on 22 in 22.

Before driving out to Ryan's, I wanted to be sure to get my run in. I had higher expectations for myself today, but again I ran only three miles.

My last three runs were each only three miles. I'm in a little rut. The problem is I don't know how to get out of it. Hopefully tomorrow, when Ryan and I run, I'll do better.

Sunday, January 23, 2022
Day 23 – 3.8 miles

It was bitter cold this morning— only about 20 degrees outside in Hershey, Pennsylvania.

I hate the cold, but I didn't hate today's run. Ryan and I ran 3.8 miles together on the steep hills around his home. On part of the run, we ran on a path that was covered in thick ice which was a particular challenge. Then on one very steep hill I had to walk briefly. Ryan was chugging forward and he didn't notice. I'm glad he didn't see me walking. I would hate for him to think that I was weak.

On our visit, we saw Ryan's chiropractic office for the first time. This was a special thrill for Laurie and I, as it shows just how far he has come in his career and his life. Pride is one of the seven deadly sins but I'm quite sure it's fine for a dad to be extremely proud of his son. Ryan gave me a great adjustment. Again, I may be his father, but I know that Ryan is an exceptional chiropractor.

We also went to a Hershey Bears hockey game. When the Bears scored their first goal, the fans threw stuffed animals onto the ice. And not just a few. Tons. Tons and tons. It was amazing and so much fun. I've never seen anything like it. By the time the toys were finished being thrown and then cleared off the ice, more than an hour had passed. In total 52,341 stuffed animals were collected. These will be donated to local charities and needy kids. What could be better than that?

Monday, January 24, 2022
  Day 24 – 4.1 miles

My lower back has been killing me. This is something that has been happening to me after long car rides, even though I had a great adjustment from Ryan yesterday.

My back especially hurt on the ride home in freezing rain and light snow and on very slow and slippery highways. I drove the first hour, but then turned over the wheel to Laurie to get us the rest of the way home.

A good driver knows when he shouldn't be driving and at that point, it was better that I wasn't the driver. Icy slick roads, especially highways, in the dark, don't thrill me.

Laurie got us home safely as I knew she would. We like to debate who is the better driver between us. Last night, she definitely was.

After we arrived home safely, Ethan and I watched what might have been Tom Brady's last NFL game. Brady and his team were down 27-3 at one point and he brought them back to tie the game at 27-27 with just a few seconds remaining. Unfortunately, the other team had a miracle of their own and won the game.

It is speculated that Tom Brady will now retire from football. Knowing that Tom Brady's football career might be over saddens Ethan and me.

I know that many people like to chop down whoever is great at the moment, and there are many Tom Brady detractors, but I look at it much differently. I believe that we should celebrate the people who achieve. We spend too much time finding reasons to discount success.

I think we'd all do a little better if we built others up rather than finding ways to take them down. Too many people spend too much time finding faults in others. None of that does a society any good.

Tuesday, January 25, 2022
    Day 25 – 5.1 miles

Today I found that spark to get through a difficult run. Nothing felt right as I ran. My legs were heavy. I felt out of sorts. I wanted to quit time after time after time again. I had nothing in the tank. I hated every single step. But, somehow I got past all of that and pushed through. I ran hard even though I had little energy and even less desire. This is what success is all about for me. Success is attained when we find ways to achieve when we least want to or when we believe that we can't. Today I was convinced that I couldn't achieve. I proved myself wrong.

I am looking forward to the end of the month. I'll feel I have accomplished something meaningful once January is completed. 340 more running days seems like an eternity, but 11 months to go doesn't seem as bad. Sometimes it's just a matter of looking at things from a different perspective.

I didn't hydrate before the run well enough, and I was wearing a number of layers of clothing, so I was sweating, a lot, and after the run, the blood returned which doesn't thrill me.

I tell myself that this doesn't scare me, but in truth it does.

Wednesday, January 26, 2022
    Day 26 – 3.60 miles

I wish I could explain the feelings I have some mornings as I awake. I love my job, but a lot has changed. This is my 24th year as a principal and for many reasons, the job itself has become much less enjoyable. I never used to dread heading into the office, but over these last few years, it seems that every single day brings some sort of crisis or change.

Where school used to be a place of happiness, I see in the eyes of the students, teachers, and parents that this is no longer the case. People are frightened and on edge, still. The patience of many, because of the great stress that they are under, is short.

I am doing everything I can to project a positive atmosphere. And I believe I am succeeding. But it's a daily challenge. And it is wearing me down.

One "tradition" of sorts that I started during on-line schooling was to record a daily motivational show for the students and the teachers on YouTube. I record a short program, each day, a few minutes long, in the spirit of Mr. Rogers. I begin each show by saying, "Let's Make Today... A Great Day!" It's been very well received in and out of the school. It sometimes takes a long time to record each show, but it's a labor of love and I believe it helps to set a positive atmosphere in the school.

***

To try to remain injury-free, I go to Physical Therapy once a month, and follow that up with a visit to my chiropractor who I have been seeing since the early 1990s. He truly is a miracle worker. The fact that I can stay so active is, in many ways, a testament to the great work he does.

My right calf had been a little sore so I didn't run in the morning and instead ran after 8:00 p.m.

Thursday, January 27, 2022
   Day 27 – 3.1 miles + 5.1 miles

Like most days, my run today came first thing in the morning. It seemed like I had just run. Because I did. Sometimes it feels like all I do is run.

With today's effort, I surpassed 100 miles for the month. In my best years, when I was a lot younger, I easily averaged more than 100 miles a month, but in the last few years, that milestone has been difficult for me to reach.

If I can do 100 miles each month this year, I'll end the year with

1,200 miles covered. I like round numbers and that's a nice big round number.

***

My Top 10 Running Songs (right now)
1. *Gonna Fly Now* – the theme song from Rocky
2. *Heart's on Fire* – John Cafferty, from Rocky IV
3. *Going The Distance* – Bill Conti from Rocky II
4. *Hall of Fame* – The Script
5. *Empire State of Mind* – Alicia Keys
6. *I Lived* – One Republic
7. *St. Elmo's Fire (Man in Motion)* – John Parr
8. *Walk* – Foo Fighters
9. *I Won't Back Down* – Tom Petty
10. *Flashdance... What a Feeling* – Irene Cara

Friday, January 28, 2022
Day 28 – 2.1 miles

I made a bad decision that I am now regretting. That decision robbed me of a good night's sleep because it was on my mind all night long.

This morning I have my annual physical. Because of this, I knew I wouldn't be able to eat or drink once I awoke. I also don't like to exercise before a doctor's visit because that might mess up my heart rate, my blood pressure, or whatever. I figure the physician needs to see me "as is."

But because I have a busy day today and because I felt great last night, I ran a blistering fast five-miles at 8:30 p.m. as a second run yesterday. After the run, I soaked in the hot tub outside basking in my glory. I was feeling strong and fit and wonderful until I came inside and was faced with bright red blood again. By the morning, things usually return to somewhat normal, but still...

I have never shared any of this with my doctor. I'm sure after all the tests today, he'll see traces of blood. I am afraid that he might tell me to stop running.

Saturday, January 29, 2022
  Day 29 – 3.1 miles

My doctor's visit went well. He is proud of me for staying in shape and not gaining weight. I actually lost a few pounds since last year (which only makes sense considering my level of activity). He didn't notice the blood yet because the practice is to leave the sample on your way out. I'm sure he'll call me in a day or two with some concern.

I ran on the treadmill as a beautiful snow fell outside. I am now at 30 miles for the week. 40-mile weeks can't be far behind. Once I start marathon training, I'll have to be doing 40-mile weeks every week. That training won't start until July, but it would be great to reach that level long before I have to. The stronger I am heading into training, the better my training should be. Good training should equal a good result in the race. We get out what we put in. Good effort most often leads to good results.

***

I noticed yesterday that the first-grade teachers hung some student reports outside their classrooms. These were the students' first attempts at writing a personal narrative.

I have seen thousands of these stories in my life. Thousands. I know what kids typically write about:
  "Losing My Tooth"
  "When I Fell Down the Stairs"
  "When Grandma Came Over."
  "Meeting Santa Claus."
  "My Birthday"
  "My First Soccer Game"
  "My Trip to Disney"
  "Christmas!"

This year, there are a host of new stories, all with the same theme:
  "Getting My Covid Shot"

Sunday, January 30, 2022
Day 30 – 7.1 miles

I sent out a Tweet today, "Hey ESPN, I'm 30-for-30!"

I decided to push it a bit today and get my first seven mile run under my belt. I didn't put on layers of clothes, I didn't run super-fast, and I drank a tall glass of water before I started. My effort was consistent and my focus was good.

I'm relieved that after the run and a long soak in the hot tub, everything was all as it should have been. (In other words, no blood.)

As motivational music from my iPod plays in my ears, I've been watching the TV show *Aerial America* as I run. The scenery in these programs is beautiful and it makes for a nice distraction. Seeing so many great scenes from across the country reminds me that there is so much I want to see and do in my life. Time is precious. I long to be traveling rather than running on a treadmill and heading off to work.

An appreciative parent just posted the following on LinkedIn:

Sunday Shoutout!

Huge shout out to the greatest principal/pitcher of all time Dr. Paul Semendinger. Earlier this month my son was anxious and worried about school. One negative COVID test and multiple trips to the nurse later, I reached out to Doc, who is always available and had a short convo about the situation. The man spent the next hour and a half between me and my son trying to help out.

We spoke for at least 20 mins and he brought up using a reward for good behavior. So I sat my son down and asked him what he wanted to do and he said I want an afternoon just the two of us.

We just spent a few hours at Dave & Busters because he made it a full week without going to the nurses office!

My family is blessed to have Dr. Sem in our lives!

Thank you!

Monday, January 31, 2022
Day 31 – 4.1 miles

Today I threw caution to the wind and ran hard while wearing a few layers of clothing. I had a big glass of water before I ran, and I stayed hydrated throughout.

Everything else was as it should be after the run. I think the key is simply to hydrate well.

One month down. 31 days into the quest completed.
***

Life can be fickle. We have a staircase that leads down to my work-out area. I took a step to head downstairs to grab my laptop before heading off to work.

But I slipped.

I teetered, I tottered... I thought I was going to catch myself, but I didn't. In an instant, I fell down our wooden stairs. Thump! Crash! Boom, Boom, Boom. That wasn't fun.

I lay on the floor at the bottom of the stairs for a moment and as-sessed myself. Nothing really hurt. Ethan yelled down, "Hey, are you okay?" (Laurie didn't hear this – she was in the shower.) I called back up the stairs, "Yup."

I seem fine, but boy, one little slip and this whole quest was almost over.

FEBRUARY

"When you choose the right kind of thoughts, you can create the running destiny you have always wanted."
Amby Burfoot

Tuesday, February 1, 2022
Day 32 – 3.1 miles

A blank calendar. That's what stared me in the face this morning. After filling January with a host of successful runs, I turned the page to a new empty month. There are still eleven blank months in front of me.

I exercised 63 different times in January. That's nuts. I ran every day, of course, but I also got some weightlifting in, rode the stationary bike, and completed my baseball throwing exercises to prepare my arm for the coming season. If nothing else, I've been very motivated in this exercise kick. The challenge will be to maintain this focus.

I'm not too much worse for wear after falling down the stairs yesterday. My right foot was sore for much of the day yesterday, but that was the only lingering effect.

Today I woke up feeling almost perfect, but I didn't want to run hard. I wanted to see how my body reacted to both yesterday's fast run and, more, my trip down my stairs.

I ran the first mile slowly, beginning at 5.0 MPH. All started well so I gradually increased the speed each tenth of a mile.

As we run, we learn about ourselves. Today I found out that I am both mentally and physically strong. After the fall, I could have easily rationalized taking the day off or running only one mile. I didn't do that. The fact that the fall didn't do any lingering damage to my body speaks to my physical strength. This gives me confidence as I move ever forward.

My doctor left a voice mail and expressed only mild concern about the blood figuring, correctly, that I had exercised before my office visit. I am pleased that he didn't immediately push the panic button.

Wednesday, February 2, 2022
   Day 33 – 5.1 miles

People sometimes ask me how I stay so motivated to do what I do athletically.

The answer is actually very simple. Over twenty years ago I made the decision to get into shape.

I remember the day exactly. We were on a family vacation in Maine and went to one of the many clothes outlets. I was going to buy a pair of pants. I had always had a 32 or 33-inch waist. The size 33 pants didn't fit. Nor did the 34's. When I went to the size 36 pants, they seemed to fit well enough. I was around 30-years old and I said, "I'm not going to start buying bigger and bigger pants. No way. I'm too young for that." I refused to buy the pants, and when we arrived home, I started exercising with more fervor and focus than I ever had before in my life.

Once I made that decision, I resolved to live up to it. Each morning, I don't allow myself a choice. As much as eating, breathing, and going to work, I require myself to be active. It has become that the daily exercise is just what I do. I don't really think about it.

On the rare days when I don't exercise, I feel different. On days when I am not active, I see myself as a failure. That seems harsh, but it's how I feel. I can't escape those feelings. I know that I let myself down and it bothers me greatly.

After decades of this routine, it has become more than a habit. It is part of who I am.

I know I have the discipline to exercise daily. Still, I don't know if I can sustain running every day. This is a huge challenge for me. And I have a long way to go.

In a very real sense, I am afraid of getting old or feeble. I can't imagine what it would be like to not be able to move well. I work out every day to try to stave off old age and to make sure that when I do get older, that I can be as active as possible.

I also know that if I take a single day off, it can easily lead to more days. I don't want to start a "consecutive days off" streak.

"I'll start again tomorrow" are very dangerous words. I don't ever want to live a life full of promises for the tomorrows that never come.

Thursday, February 3, 2022
Day 34 – 4.1 miles

There is a stereotype that runners are excellent eaters; that we consume only healthy foods. It's not true. I'm not a great eater. I never have been. My food of choice, almost all of the time, is pizza. I love pizza. I could eat pizza for every meal every day for the rest of my life. I don't think pizza is unhealthy, but it's certainly not the best food to eat as often as I probably do.

I try. I really do try. But it's difficult for me. I don't like many vegetables. And because I am so busy and always on the run (literally and figuratively), I don't make much time to eat. I consume a lot of energy bars. That's how I try to get nutrients into my body. It's not the best way. To begin each day, I take a multi-vitamin and drink a large glass of water with Metamucil. I believe the daily fiber helps with my blood sugar levels.

Years ago, my long-term sugar numbers put me in the pre-diabetic range. I made a lot of changes to my diet then, but it's still something I feel I need to monitor on a daily basis through a morning check of my glucose. This approach was recommended to me by a nutritionist. For a few years my doctor agreed with this and prescribed a once-a-day daily glucose monitoring system for me. But last year at my annual exam, he saw that my numbers had been good for a while and stopped the prescriptions.

In the follow-up phone call following my check-up last week, my doctor noted that my sugar numbers were rising. He agreed to re-order the daily testing regimen. My goal each day is to be under 100 on the glucose monitor. I still had some old strips and began my daily testing yesterday. I need this. If I know I'm testing myself, it makes it easier for me to resist sweets or bad foods. It's a way I hold myself accountable.

I am certain that if I didn't check my sugar levels each morning and I didn't run and exercise like a madman, I'd be a diabetic by now.

I am also afraid I'm going to hit a wall soon. I am finding it extremely difficult to stay motivated to run each day. As I covered the miles today, I listened to a little-known Queen song titled *Fight From The Inside*. The message from this song helped me. I was reminded throughout that the challenge to complete a task always comes from within.

Friday, February 4, 2022
　　Day 35- 4.1 miles

I don't eat well and last night I ate even worse. I went out with five of my best friends to dinner and ate steak and French fries and onion rings. Along the way I imbibed way too much.

In a social setting like this, imbibing means drinking soda. If I drink alcohol, which isn't often, it's only at home alone with Laurie. I never drink in public. Most of my friends have never seen me consuming alcohol. It's rare even for my own children to see me drinking.

When I am with friends, or anyone, I don't want to cloud my judgement by being compromised because of alcohol. I also never want to get behind the wheel of a car with even a trace of alcohol in my system. I can't imagine the embarrassment it would cause if I lost my license.

Instead of driving drunk, I drove home strung out on syrupy sugary Pepsi.

All that bad food and sugar brought my glucose level well over 100. I blew it yesterday and now I have to be smarter.

***

I awoke at 4:00, as I do most mornings, answering e-mails, writing, getting my blog ready, and preparing myself for the day. I didn't start running because I had a sense that the phone might ring as the weather outside is bad and due to get worse – rain, ice, and sleet. If they call for an early dismissal, I need to be available for my staff in case any questions come up.

No matter how many times we do these things, questions always come up.

Once the call for an early dismissal came, I e-mailed my staff with some reminders and jumped on the TM knowing I'd still have time to answer any last-minute questions.

Saturday, February 5, 2022
Day 36 – 2.1 miles

The running streak became a real drag again today. When I'm only running for the sake of simply getting the run in, and not for good hard vigorous exercise, it becomes a chore. Today my running was a chore.

With each run, I always hope to capture the elation that came as I ran my first marathon, in New York City, in 2002. There was nothing like it. It was an experience I didn't expect and the euphoria it brought still lingers today.

I knew that there were people who cheered for the runners in the marathon, but I never expected the absolute magnitude of it all in New York City. Millions of people lined the streets. There were bands and people with noise makers. It was a carnival-like atmosphere. As I took part in the race, I felt that the crowds were all cheering for me. I still sometimes imagine they were.

There's a part of me that seeks to find a way to recapture the elation I felt in my first marathon every single time I run.

Sunday, February 6, 2022
Day 37 – 4.1 miles

Today I crossed a milestone as this was my 37th consecutive day of running. That puts me at 10% of the calendar year. This seems like a big step. I feel this is something significant.

We accomplish big goals by breaking them down into smaller ones.

Tonight, we'll head to the Cheesecake Factory to celebrate Laurie's birthday. Laurie's actual birthday is tomorrow, but we're celebrating tonight. As we wait for our table, we'll walk through the Barnes & Noble's next door. I hope they have my Yankees book. If they do, I'll secretly autograph it.

Monday, February 7, 2022
Day 38 – 3.1 miles

My beautiful wife turns 54 today. She is five months older than me. When we started dating, back in high school, she could drive before I could.

Back then it was better to be older. Now, not so much.

Tuesday, February 8, 2022
Day 39 – 5.1 miles

Feeling very strong, I pushed very hard, getting a five-miler completed in under 43 minutes. This was the first time I broke 43:00 in a five-miler run since 2016. Six long years. I used to be able to break 35 minutes routinely, but age, and the surgery changed a lot.

***

After work today, I'm giving blood. I give blood as often as I can. When I go in, they ask, "What are you giving today?" I always respond, "What do you need?"

Lately they have been asking for platelets or double-red cells. I'm happy to give.

Wednesday, February 9, 2022
Day 40 – 3.1 miles

Since I gave blood yesterday, I took it easy today. They told me to wait 24-hours before exercising. They don't realize that I'm Superman. I waited 14 hours. Close enough.

***

I have been thinking a lot about my job. I love my school and the people who make up the school community, but I often wonder if my best days are behind me. We had a situation earlier this school year that caused many of us on staff a great deal of stress and angst. In a school replete with seasoned outstanding teachers, much of what we saw, and worked to solve, was unlike anything we'd ever before encountered. In the end, we did some great work but there were times in that process when I wondered if the job was going to kill me. My father was always in good shape, and he had a heart attack in his early fifties. All of this got me thinking more and more about retirement. I always thought 2023 would be my last year, but that day might come a year sooner than I had originally planned. I would hate to go, but, more and more I am realizing that my best days are probably behind me.

Thursday, February 10, 2022
　　Day 41 – 4.1 miles

Yesterday we had a meeting for the elementary principals that lasted all afternoon. I greatly dislike long meetings. We have a few meetings like this per month. It's been this way my whole administrative career across numerous school districts.

The topics all seem to run together, and have, forever. We end up talking about the same things meeting after meeting, year after year. Yesterday we talked about grammar and word study units and mid-year placement tests. Those things are important, of course, but I don't believe they should be the primary focus of our efforts or energy.

One thing that's rarely on the list of discussion topics is students. Our meetings are primarily focused on curriculum and standards, test scores and programs. We talk a lot about rubrics. And there are always new state mandates and procedures to review.

I will miss a lot about my job when I retire. I will not miss sitting in long meetings essentially about nothing.

Today I did my fastest four-miler since 2016. My personality is such that I am driven to keep getting better. Faster, to me, means better.

Friday, February 11, 2022
　　Day 42 – 2.1 miles

This is one of the ironies of running. Today's run was very difficult. It took all of my willpower and effort to get through it. After two fast runs this week, I had nothing in the tank today.

I consider these two-mile efforts to be almost cheating. The result makes it look like I took it easy today, but today's run was, in some ways, more difficult than the fast ones I've accomplished recently. The miles don't often show how much effort one has to give. Sometimes it is more difficult to run one or two miles than it is to run five or six. That might not make sense to a non-runner, but it is absolutely true.

***

The other day there was a discussion among the elementary school principals about Valentine's Day. Some schools are going to tell the students that they can only bring cards—no treats, no small gifts, no lollypops or sweetheart candies—nothing. Not even a pencil or an eraser.

I'm going rogue on this and am going to allow Valentine's Day to be whatever it is. I'm not putting rules on what children can or can't attach to their Valentine's cards. I refuse to take away more of the joys of childhood from the students.

Haven't the kids had enough taken away already?

Saturday, February 12, 2022
Day 43 – 3.40 miles

We have had two consecutive days with spring-like weather. As a result, I was able to break away from the treadmill and run outside.

I thought the run would be enjoyable. I thought getting outside would be great. It wasn't. Everything hurt. Even though it was 57 degrees, it felt cold. I wanted to greatly enjoy this run, but I didn't.

Sunday, February 13, 2022
  Day 44 – 7.1 miles

Today is Super Bowl Sunday!

My favorite Super Bowl was in 1982 when the Washington Redskins rolled over the Miami Dolphins. My favorite football player, John Riggins, a great running back, was the star of that game. He wore #44.

Today was my 44th consecutive day running.

Since Ethan and I are going to eat too much junk food later as we watch the game, I figured a good long run would make sense. I ran my fastest 7-miler since... 2016.

After a few poor runs, it felt great to have a good run again today. I wish I could sustain this success and be this strong of a runner every single day. Unfortunately, running doesn't work like that. Each day and each run bring their own challenges, successes, or failures.

Monday, February 14, 2022
  Day 45 – 4.1 miles

During my run this morning, I was thinking about trophies and the like. The 2021 New York City Marathon was the 50th running of that iconic race. I ran that marathon. Everyone who completed the race received a big gold-like finisher's medal.

After the race, I was at a snack stand purchasing a candy bar. The guy at the counter saw the medal around my neck, looked up at me, looked back at the medal and then said in a questioning tone, "You won?"

I smiled. I said that I did, sort of, but that I was sure that at least 20,000 people finished ahead of me.

Tuesday, February 15, 2022
   Day 46 – 4.1 miles

Running every day with headphones probably isn't good for my hearing. When I run hard, I sometimes play the music much too loudly. The motivation from the music helps me accomplish my goals, but I worry that I might be doing irreparable harm to my long-term hearing.

I do take a break every mile from the music. At a little past the half-way point each mile, I pray. I do this with every mile I run, at least when I run alone. It's part of what I do. I turn off the music on my iPod when I pray so I have no distractions.

Most often I simply recite *The Lord's Prayer* quietly to myself, but as I say the words, I try to think about them and how they apply to my life. I use this prayer to connect with God, but also to think of the core values I am reciting. The prayer reminds us that we often fall short ("forgive us our trespasses") and it also encourages us to be understanding of others when they stumble ("as we forgive those who trespass against us").

For the most part, I run alone, but I invite God to come along with me, so, in some ways, I'm never alone. I usually run a little better and feel a little stronger after I pray.

Wednesday, February 16, 2022
   Day 47 – 3.35 miles

The saying, "slow and steady wins the race" is true much of the time, but not always. This morning, I set out to do a slow five miles, but sometimes "nice and easy" turns into "tedious and difficult." Sometimes when I go too slowly, I lose my focus and my willingness to keep running. That is what happened today. I got just past three miles and could not keep going. I hit "Stop" on the treadmill and that ended my effort.

"Slow and steady" in a sense lost the race for me. I lost my focus and fell short of the goal I set for myself. Maybe this is the wrong attitude to have. I did go three miles, but it wasn't what I wanted to do, and that's frustrating. There are times when I expect too much of myself and as I get older, I find that I can't quite do what I think I used to. Today was a good example of this.

Thursday, February 17, 2022
Day 48 – 4.1 miles

I again wanted to go five miles, but on my fourth mile, I felt my legs starting to give out a little. I pushed through to finish the mile and stopped. Yesterday I felt like a bit of a failure. Today, because I felt something not quite right in my legs, I believe I am being smart. In this case, discretion is definitely the better part of valor.

I have this fear that I'm going hurt myself to the point where I have to stop running. That would be a disaster.

I have come this far, and although I have a very long way to go, I do not plan on quitting. I need to accomplish this goal this year. I'm not getting any younger. If not now, when?

***

We had a very important meeting yesterday with select administrators in the district and we determined that once the state's mask mandate is over that we will go back to pre-pandemic norms. There will be no more restrictions. Schools will return to doing things the ways we always used to. I cannot wait to tell my staff. This will bring a lot of energy back into the building.

We're going to party like it's 2019.

Friday, February 18, 2022
Day 49 – 4.15 miles

Right now, I feel like I am in a good place. I am pushing forward each day. While not every run has been fun, and some have been especially challenging, I am continuing my streak. On days like this, I believe that I will be able to run all year – and maybe forever!

Running is a sport that offers a great deal of feedback. My body continually tells me how I am doing. My efforts are also affirmed on a daily basis when I log my runs on my exercise calendar and on Strava - an online portal where I record all of my runs.

It's all about moving forward.

Saturday, February 19, 2022
Day 50 – 5.0 miles

And this is the problem I face each morning and each day. Yesterday was great, but yesterday is gone and today I struggled to get motivated to run. I woke up thinking of so many things I want to do, including relaxing, but this task does not allow me to bask in the glory of yesterday. Each day presents a new challenge and a new struggle.

After only one and a half miles, I couldn't keep going. My motivation was completely gone. Not wanting or allowing myself to quit, I developed a different plan. Since I didn't seem to have the focus to run for longer lengths of time, I broke the run into shorter and faster segments with small walking breaks in between. I ran:

1.50 miles at 9:43 pace then
1.25 miles at 9:09 pace then
1.00 miles at 8:43 pace then
0.75 miles at 8:35 pace and I finished with
0.50 miles at 8:14 pace.

All told, it was five miles in total running. That's how to make something out of nothing.

Sunday, February 20, 2022
Day 51 – 2.1 miles

I had two things on my mind as I ran today.

First, I know that I have listened to too much music on my head-phones, so I ran without music on the TM. I sort of enjoyed the "freedom."

Second, since I have a few days off for a mid-February break, we're heading to Boston to see our son Alex and his girlfriend Perri. Laurie and I wanted to get out of the house quickly, so I didn't want to waste too much time on the TM delaying our trip. I usually feel discouraged after a two-mile effort, but not today. I have more im-portant miles to cover as we head to Massachusetts.

Monday, February 21, 2022
    Day 52 – 2.5 miles

This is, in many ways, what I look forward to in retirement. I love traveling, seeing my family, and finding new places to run.

I especially love running in cities.

Laurie and I are staying at The Kendall in Cambridge, an old fire-house which is now a boutique hotel. The hotel is just over the bridge from Boston.

This morning I bundled up (it's in the low 30's) and headed out for a run. As I left the comfort of the warm hotel room, and my wife, one of my first thoughts was, "This whole running everyday experience is a drag." I would have much preferred to stay inside.

But once I started out, it became a great run. I covered only 2.5 miles, but, in some ways, it seemed like I ran forever. As I began, I quickly came upon the Longfellow Bridge that crosses the Charles River. Alex took us on a 12-mile walk of Boston last summer and I remem-bered it all immediately. I crossed over and into Boston and found a trail that paralleled the river. They call this area the Esplanade. It's a quiet place for recreation and, even on this cold morning was filled with many people running, roller blading, and walking.

I have always loved running in city parks; places where the people of the city come together, almost as one. It's almost as if we all know each other, even though we don't. I'm sure I ran with a huge smile on my face.

I love exploring cities. When we travel, I most often make time (usually in the early morning) to run. I enjoy discovering new places in this manner. I have encountered and seen so much more than I would have ever seen if I was in a car, bus, or subway.

Once, in Hiroshima, Japan, as I ran near the A-Bomb Dome, I came across a group of Japanese school children singing. I couldn't help but be drawn into the sound—quiet melodious voices singing of peace in a place devastated by the horrors of war. The songs were sung in Japanese, but I could tell from the music that the songs were ones of hope. I stopped running and took it all in. It was one of the most beautiful experiences of my entire life.

Tuesday, February 22, 2022
Day 53 – 5.0 miles

This morning I was once again out in the cold early morning Boston air. I ran again on the Charles River Esplanade and then crossed over the Arthur Fiedler Bridge and went deeper into Boston. I quickly saw the Boston Common and, off in the distance, the George Washington Statue which I ran to. On my way back, I returned to the Esplanade, came across a statue of George Patton, and headed back over the Longfellow Bridge.

Once I was back in Cambridge, since I had a little more energy, I ran around the MIT campus. Yesterday, Alex, Perri, Laurie, and I walked around Harvard Square. I didn't attend an Ivy League school, but by being on those campuses I feel a lot smarter right now.

***

The Longfellow Bridge intrigues me. On the Cambridge side of the river, people have put medals and trophies in the rafters under the bridge. I have no idea why they do this or where the tradition began, but it's things like this, first "discovered" (in our family, at least) by Alex that so intrigue me. All told, there must be hundreds of trophies of all different types stacked under the bridge.

Many years ago, I played for a super competitive local softball team in a men's league. We won a few championships, but one year, we lost the last game of the championship in the last inning. Our coach was given the second-place trophies, but instead of handing them out to the players, he threw them into the woods. The town stopped awarding trophies to the winners (and runners-up) after that. We soon won another championship, and since the town didn't award us trophies for our efforts, we purchased our own.

I have all of these trophies in my office at school. When the students see them, they think I am some sort of superstar athlete. I usually don't correct them.

Wednesday, February 23, 2022
Day 54 – 3.0 miles

Laurie and I arrived home and I ran outside since it was over sixty degrees. Today was the first day that really felt like spring. I have enjoyed running free of music and the treadmill these last few days.

As I ran, my feet and legs felt the pounding of the roads and sidewalks. It usually takes my body some time to acclimate to the pounding they take outside. The roads at home seem harder and less forgiving than in other places. We also live in an area comprised of many hills. These also take some getting used to. It seems they are all always up hill. I can't explain it.

As I ran, I thought of the title for a novel I should write, *The Hills of Home*.

Sometimes I get my best ideas when I run.

***

Today I reached the longest consecutive running streak I ever reached before—53 days.

The last time I tried to run every day for a year, in 2018, I did a lot of one-mile runs. Over those 53 days, I ran a grand total of only 101 miles. My heart wasn't into it. I kept trying to find the easy way out and a lot of that streak felt like I was cheating in some way.

This time it's different. I have had no one-mile runs. To date, I have covered over 200 miles this year. If I keep this pace, I'll reach 1,400 miles by the end of the year. I do like round numbers but I doubt I'll go that far. To me that sounds crazy right now.

Thursday, February 24, 2022
Day 55 – 3.1 miles

Today it was back to the treadmill and also back to work.

I am enjoying this new approach of running without music blasting in my ears. It's interesting, one would think that it would be easier to run on the treadmill without the distractions from the music, but that isn't the case for me. The music is a great motivator—often-times, the louder, the better.

Now, without the music, I'm thinking about a lot more things. For example, I am actually more focused on my running which, in a cra-zy way, makes the efforts more difficult. I notice every single thing that feels uncomfortable or that slightly hurts.

I won't forgo music on all my runs, I'd miss it too much. But I en-joyed the relative silence today. That being said, I'll have to watch that Rocky montage again one day soon. That also never fails to motivate me!

Friday, February 25, 2022
Day 56 – 4.1 miles

I love my job, the school, the kids, the teachers, the families... so, so, so much, but I'm starting to feel like it is more of a struggle than ever before to be at the top of my game. So much has changed these last few years. I am working as hard as ever, but there are so many challenges that were never present before. We have unique issues with students that are probably due to the fact that they missed so much school and socialization these last few years. I think we've done so many children a great disservice by isolating them. The teachers are working hard, the parents too. I have a great school community, but so much is different in so many ways. People have been, and are, on edge. My job is giving me less joy than ever before. I still believe I am very effective as a principal, but I sometimes I wonder how much longer I can keep this up – working 24/7, literally. I wonder what it would be like to get out while I'm still at my best, or at least the best I can be right now. I thought of a Hall of Fame baseball player the other day...

On September 28, 1960, in the bottom of the eighth inning, Ted Williams came to bat for the Boston Red Sox. In what was the last at bat of his career, Williams promptly hit a long fly over the outfield fence, circled the bases, and disappeared into the dugout. Teddy Ballgame, as he was known, ended his great career with a home run.

That's how to go out on top!

Saturday, February 26, 2022
   Day 57 – 3.1 miles

We are remodeling our basement at home. I had decorated the walls of this area with the bibs from all of the races I have run. After each race, I'd add the newest race number bib to the wall. There were over a hundred of these making a border around the entire room. I loved looking at them and remembering each of the races – the good, the bad, the successes, and the ones where I didn't do so well. To prepare for the room to be painted, I had to remove my race numbers this week. I put them all in a box and I feel like part of my life has been put away forever.

***

I ran fast today and broke eight-minute-miles. I was convinced this was my fastest run of the year, but it wasn't. It's all becoming a blur.

Sunday, February 27, 2022
Day 58 – 1.17 miles

The running streak is in jeopardy. I have prided myself in not having any one-mile runs this year. I have one now.

Earlier this week, as we traveled to and from Boston, my back hurt a lot after the long car rides. The pain eventually lessened, but it hadn't gone away. This morning my back hurt worse than ever.

I got on the treadmill after doing some back exercises that Ryan taught me, but I wasn't feeling quite right. After finishing one mile, my back seized up. The pain was tremendous. I grabbed the rails of the treadmill and tried to continue, but the pain did not let up and I had to stop.

I'm not sure what tomorrow will bring. The pain comes in waves and seizes my whole body. I know only one thing, I'm going to try to push through this for the sake of the running streak. I do not want to quit. I cannot quit. I have to make it through this year. When I explain all of this, Laurie rolls her eyes at me. She's seen me battle through all sorts of injuries. She's long since given up telling me that the smart thing to do is stop. If the Achilles tears didn't stop me (at least for a year or two), this shouldn't. Ryan, Alex, and Ethan just see or hear about me struggling through and think, "Yup, that's what Dad does."

Monday, February 28, 2022
Day 59 – 2.1 miles

Late in the day yesterday I called Ryan who talked Ethan, who works in a physical therapy office, through some manipulations that he could do on my back. In essence we did remote chiropractic. This helped make me feel better and it allowed me to get my run in. Sometimes I get so busy that I cannot make the time to get to my chiropractor and yesterday was a Sunday, so he was closed. I'm glad I have this remote option available.

MARCH

"The harder you work, the harder it is to surrender."
Vince Lombardi

Tuesday, March 1, 2022
    Day 60 – 3.1 miles

Two full calendars of runs.

Ten empty ones...

***

After a visit to my chiropractor yesterday, I felt slightly better. This morning I was able to do three miles, but it was a slow and tedious effort. I am back to listening to music as I run. The thought of running in silence would make this whole experience even worse. At least the music is a distraction.

Wednesday, March 2, 2022
    Day 61 – 4.1 miles

My back is slowly feeling better. These slow runs have been tedious.

Running is both a mental and a physical challenge. If we're in the correct frame of mind, we can often run through all sorts of pain. It isn't the smartest thing to do, but it can be done. Most runners run through a lot of pain. It's interesting, people often see runners as weak, they're often portrayed as skinny weaklings, but it takes tremendous will and strength to push forward mile after mile.

One year, I ran the New York City Marathon with a stress fracture in my foot. And, before my surgery, I ran the 2018 race with tears in my Achilles tendon. These are things that should debilitate me, but somehow I can compartmentalize them and still focus on getting through a race. I am not unique in this – in any way. This is the tale of many runners.

I am proud of myself when I can push through pain, but I wonder if it is good for my long-term physical well-being. In the short term, I don't see another choice, especially this year.

I rationalize that when I am old, I would rather be hobbled from injuries sustained from being too active in my younger years than hobbled by a failing body that was not active enough.

Thursday, March 3, 2022
    Day 62 – 3.13 miles

Each day I'm running a little faster despite some lingering pain in my lower back.

I had thought about pushing another mile, but I'm having an early morning Faculty Meeting before school to discuss the first day back without the mask mandate which will be next Monday, and I wanted to get to the office quickly. Masks will now be optional for all staff and all students. I will not be wearing a mask. This is the next big step towards normalcy.

Friday, March 4, 2022
    Day 63 – 4.1 miles

There is a certain euphoria that comes from running. Some people call this the "runner's high," but I reject that terminology. It has nothing to do with getting "high."

We live in a society where many are fascinated by the idea of drug highs. I think this gives the euphoria that comes with running the wrong connotation. A drug high comes from a foreign substance introduced into the body. The runner's high, on the other hand, comes only through vigorous work. These great feelings are totally natural. They come through the endorphins one's own body creates naturally. In every way it's the polar opposite of a high brought on by drugs.

For me the euphoria comes when I push my body beyond what I think it can do, either by running faster, farther, or both. When I find myself in a rut during a run, I try to remind myself that I am strong. I try to tell myself that I can withstand the pain or whatever it is I'm suffering through. I find that over time, the pains that accompany a run usually go away. I find that the key to success in running is often pushing hard when the task seems most difficult.

This is where my good feelings come from. That's my "runner's high."

Saturday, March 5, 2022
   Day 64 – 3.1 miles

I keep thinking about those who went out on top.

The date was September 21, 1955. Tens of thousands flocked to Yankee Stadium in the Bronx, New York, not to watch a baseball game, but to see a heavyweight fight. Archie Moore, who had won 149 professional fights, was set to battle against the great Rocky Marciano.

The two sluggers battled for nine rounds, but in that round Marciano knocked out Moore to win the fight. Marciano's win gave him a perfect professional record of 49-0. He'd never fight again.

Rocky Marciano was one who went out on top.

Sunday, March 6, 2022
   Day 65 – 3.0 miles

The following have been the paces of my runs this week:

Monday: 12:00 minute miles
Tuesday: 11:19 minute miles
Wednesday: 10:53 minute miles
Thursday: 10:20 minute miles
Friday: 9:42 minute miles
Saturday: 9:08 minute miles

Today I finally got outside again and ran 8:43 minute miles. I call this progress. I used to run sub eight-minute-miles regularly. I am very pleased when I can still approach that pace.

Today was Day 65. It was a good number; another milestone. I have exactly 300 days to go. This gives me confidence.

Monday, March 7, 2022
Day 66 – 5.1 miles

A body in motion stays in motion. A body at rest stays at rest.

I am afraid of becoming that body at rest.

Tuesday, March 8, 2022
Day 67 – 3.1 miles

Yesterday was a great day at school. I would say that 85% of the kids and teachers were without masks. At drop-off many parents said, "It's great to finally see your smiling face again!"

For me, it was great to see the students' faces again – real live smiles. It's been two years since we saw the faces of the children we teach.
***

I was thinking about my "mile prayers" as I ran today.

I believe God listens to us, but he doesn't answer all our prayers, wishes, or hopes in ways we often understand. He doesn't operate like a magic genie. We don't always know why certain things occur, but I'm sure they often happen for a reason. That doesn't mean that everything is predestined. God gave us free will. Still, I find that the things in my life tend to go better when I involve God into my thoughts and decisions.

Running provides me with the time necessary, away from all other distractions, to let God into my life. The prayers I recite help me feel closer to him. I believe the prayers help my runs. I also believe they help me in my life.

Wednesday, March 9, 2022
Day 68 – 3.1 miles

Today I got my first taste of what it might feel like to announce my retirement.

A reminder came to sign-up for my local softball team. I have played in this league for 19 seasons, but since I'll be on two baseball teams this year, I decided not to play softball. A man can only do so much.

I sent a message to the team thanking them for our years together and announced that I won't be playing this year.

And then I cried. I'm not good at good-byes.

Thursday, March 10, 2022
Day 69 – 3.1 miles

When it is all over, I'll pride myself in knowing I made a difference.

A veteran teacher just sent the following to me,

> *"Thank You for being the best principal I've ever had the privilege to work with! I know you always give the staff credit for the uniqueness of Hawes School BUT it's because of you that*

we are able to do what we do."

I needed to receive that note because things had not been great at work. There have been some difficult situations I have to deal with and I have not been sleeping well. Yesterday I was up at 2:45 a.m. Today I slept in... I made it to 3:00 a.m.

I'm exhausted, but getting the runs in. I'm plodding along day after day right now. I'd like to find a way to run and sleep at the same time.

Friday, March 11, 2022
    Day 70 – 3.1 miles

Tonight is one of my favorite nights of the school year as it's Dads' Night.

Dads' Night has been part of the schools since 1944. In this, the fathers put on a vaudeville-like program for the children filled with silly skits and lots of fun. There will be shows tonight and tomorrow. The auditorium will be packed wall-to-wall for both shows.

I play the saxophone in the Dads' Night Band. Just like the rush I derive from running well, I love playing rock-and roll with the dads. I am not an accomplished musician, but for two nights a year, I get to feel like a rock star.

Saturday, March 12, 2022
    Day 71 – 4.1 miles

A band called Motorcycle had a hit a number of years ago called *As The Rush Comes*. I listened to that song over and over as I ran on the TM today. I helped me stay focused enough to run under nine-minute-miles.

I wonder how well I'd be doing if that back pain hadn't set me back a few weeks ago. But now, my right arm, my pitching arm, started killing me yesterday. I haven't been throwing, so it can't be from baseball. I don't know how this happened, but it could be a huge problem.

Injuries to one's legs and feet and knees scare runners. Injuries to one's throwing arm scares the life out of a pitcher. A fifty-three-year-old pitcher is already operating on borrowed time.

Sunday, March 13, 2022
Day 72 – 5.1 miles

Yesterday was brutally cold. Today too. Winter is holding on which is annoying because on the weekends, when I have a little more time, I really want to escape the treadmill and run outside.

I was able to run my fastest five-miler this year. I have now had back-to-back fast runs. This encourages me a great deal. My running is coming back to where it had been before the back injury.

Now, if my right arm felt better, I'd be really happy.

Monday, March 14, 2022
Day 73 – 3.1 miles

One of the interesting aspects of the sport of running is that a runner never knows how his body will respond from day to day. Each run is different. There have been times when I have been in peak marathon shape and found it a struggle to run even a few miles. Conversely, there have been times when the distance of my runs far exceeded what I thought I was capable of.

I have been running for decades and have run tens of thousands of miles, and yet, so much of this sport is still a mystery to me. I am continually trying to figure out how to become more consistent from one day to the next. Earlier last week, I was exhausted. Yesterday I was fast and strong and able. Today I was plodding and slow and I lacked confidence.

I finished my workout today wondering where the strong person I was yesterday had disappeared to.

Tuesday, March 15, 2022
  Day 74 – 6.1 miles

The Ides of March have arrived and for one of the few times in my career, I keep wondering if Brutus is going to appear in my office with a dagger. There seems to be a new dynamic at play in schools all across this area. I have talked to many colleagues in the region, and most are experiencing a similar concern.

Abraham Lincoln once commented about the inability to please all of the people all of the time. Right now, there are two diametrically opposed forces at play pushing, fervently, against each other. There are members of the community who want the schools to be completely as they were before the lockdowns. They want all of the old programs and experiences to be back and running immediately.

At the same time, there is an equally concerned collection of people who are asking for more safeguards to be put into practice. They are not pleased that we are returning (step-by-step) to normal operations. They feel we are putting their children at risk.

It seems that getting back to normal is not going to happen smoothy, nor easily.

To compound this, possibly because so many people have been isolated for so long, there is an intolerance for the opposing viewpoints. In short, people are still on edge, for any number of reasons. Some are taking those frustrations out on the schools.

I don't believe Abraham Lincoln ever mentioned pleasing none of the people all of the time.

***

I wanted to run a good distance today because my weight has ballooned a bit. Stress doesn't do good things for the body. I am pleased that I was able to complete six miles, my longest run since February 13.

That seems like a lifetime ago.

Wednesday, March 16, 2022
Day 75 – 3.1 miles

A figurative bomb was dropped yesterday at work. Our new superintendent, who has been fantastic, called a special meeting with the administrative team yesterday and announced that he is leaving the district at the end of the school year.

Our previous superintendent, who had served for thirteen years, left last year amid some of the turmoil that we've all lived through. That makes two quality superintendents leaving our district in two years. That's not good. Quality organizations need quality leaders.

I didn't let my intentions be known, but as everything becomes more chaotic around me, I am certain that my decision, to retire, which I have been thinking about more and more, and one that I think I'll announce soon, is the correct one.

***

I'm donating platelets later, so I didn't push the distance or my pace today.

This was my 75th consecutive day of running. It some ways it feels like I just started. In others, it feels like it was my 750th day of running.

Thursday, March 17, 2022
Day 76 – 4.1 miles

Sometimes it's the memories of my greatest runs that help me get through my toughest running challenges.

The best marathon I ever ran was in Chicago in 2006. I was still young, not yet even 40-years-old, and was strong and fast. I knew I was ready to have a great race.

I wore a shirt with my first name on the front and received tons of cheers as I flew through the neighborhoods around Wrigley Field. The cheering was constant, and unlike in other races, so many people were cheering for me:

"Go Paul!"
"You look great, Paul!"
"You rock, Paul!"
"Yeah! Paul!!"

It went on like this for blocks, maybe a mile or two…

A runner next to me asked, "Is this your town?" I said, "No."

He replied, "It is today."

Friday, March 18, 2022
Day 77 – 4.1 miles

I ran fast today, but that knot in my back started hurting again.

Saturday, March 19, 2022
Day 78 – 2.1 miles, 3.0 miles

I should have tried doing this running every day task years ago because I feel my body breaking down. Maybe I'm too old to do this. Still, I cannot allow myself to stop.

I actually ran twice today. First, I did an easy run on the TM because it was raining. Later, because it was beautiful and warm, I got outside. I usually don't like to quit a run until I get back home, but today I stopped at three miles. I had to walk about a mile to get home, but that was fine. The warm air and the quietness of being alone outside helped me find some time to think.

Sunday, March 20, 2022
Day 79 – 4.0 miles

I am tired today. I got outside, but again didn't have much spring in my step.

There are a number of major issues I am dealing with at work, and I believe the energy I'm expending on these things is wiping me out. I'm not the same person I usually am.

It is frustrating when I'm not full of positive energy. I am better than this. I need to find that inner resolve to get back to where I need to be in all aspects of my life.

Monday, March 21, 2022
Day 80 – 5.1 miles

The life of being a runner is a strange thing. Today I woke up with great confidence and got on the treadmill ready to run fast. Everything seemed to work great and I finished the run at faster than nine-minute-mile pace.

I get frustrated when I follow a great run with a poor one, but when I bounce back from a difficult run with great results like today, I feel new energy.

I need to figure out how to sustain this.

Tuesday, March 22, 2022
Day 81 – 3.1 miles

I yearn to be outside more, but the weather isn't cooperating.

***

Last night Laurie, Ethan, and I spent the evening organizing our remodeled rooms downstairs. I started assembling some of the furniture we recently purchased from IKEA, but was soon interrupted by an important phone call.

Laurie and Ethan then spent time undoing what I had started. I had done everything reversed. This is often how I build things—incorrectly.

Wednesday, March 23, 2022
Day 82 – 4.1 miles

I wanted to quit my run early today but found the determination to reach four miles. On many runs I have the desire to stop. When I don't, when I push through the desire to quit, I know I am accomplishing something.

***

At an administrative meeting recently, a district leader was presenting concern of hers about teachers wearing jeans to work. The administrator felt it was unprofessional for teachers to dress in this fashion.

It was an ironic presentation. While this administrator was sharing this very serious concern of hers, she was wearing a denim jacket. I had to laugh to myself. I guess jeans are only bad from the waist down.

Thursday, March 24, 2022
Day 83 – 4.1 miles

Each run builds upon the ones that came before. I believe I am getting stronger, but I have only been able to reach thirty miles in a week twice this year. I haven't reached that total since February. I am a little frustrated because I would have thought that I would have had many more long runs completed by this point in the year. I am covering the miles, but my overall physical fitness doesn't seem to be improving much (or at all) since I started.

Friday, March 25, 2022
   Day 84 – 4.1 miles

Last evening, I had a book talk at a local library that went very well. About twenty people showed up which is a big crowd for me.

I once did a library book talk and no one showed up. This was for one of my *Principal Sam* picture books for kids. I sat in the children's section alone. A little kid was playing on the floor. I said, "Want me to read a book to you." He said, "YES!" So, I read my book to him and then packed up my things and went home.

Another time, I was chosen among many authors from across the state to showcase my books at a minor league baseball game. Laurie, Alex, and Ethan came with me. We carried hundreds of books into the stadium. I told everyone that we'd have a lighter load to carry on the way out after the game. It didn't turn out that way at all. I didn't sell a single book.

***

Our pastor is ill. He called and asked me to serve as the minister in church this coming Sunday.

I also found that we are going to have a teacher shortage due to illnesses.

***

It seems like each day, there are new challenges that people are hoping I can solve. So far, I am succeeding. I wonder if it is all the running that is keeping me sane.

Saturday, March 26, 2022
Day 85 – 2.1 miles

The streak almost ended today. I couldn't find any time to get on the treadmill until after 8:30 p.m. and wasn't able to maintain the effort to reach thirty miles for the week, which I had thought would have been easy to reach at this point. I feel like I failed.

In a situation like this, I think back to each of my runs. I know that if I had been a little stronger, and run a little longer, I wouldn't have fallen short. But this week, I did.

I set goals to motivate myself and to help me keep my focus. Without goals, each run seems insignificant, but when each run is part of a bigger plan, it creates a level of accountability that I feel responsible to meet. I'll strive to do better next week.

Sunday, March 27, 2022
Day 86 – 4.1 miles

I did a fair job leading the two church services today. During the first service, though, I made one big mistake; a misstep that is unexplainable.

In the service, as I was leading the congregation in *The Lord's Prayer*, my mind went blank. I lost my place. I forgot the words. I ended up standing there awkwardly as everyone else finished in their own cadence.

This, of course, made no sense. I recite *The Lord's Prayer* during each mile when I run. I also say it every night before going to sleep. How I forgot the words is beyond me. It was an embarrassing moment. After the service as I greeted the congregation, I apologized for totally blanking out. They were all forgiving and most gave me huge smiles.

***

Before the service, the idea of rest thwarted my run. As I was reaching four miles, I decided that I'd rather sit in the hot tub than run an extra mile or two.

I need to be better than that.

Monday, March 28, 2022
    Day 87 – 5.1 miles

Today, I ran hard and fast and true. I set a new "fastest five-miler since 2016."

I think one thing that helped me run fast today was this sense that I was trying to run away from embarrassing myself in church yesterday.

Tuesday, March 29, 2022
    Day 88 – 4.1 miles

I pushed through for an uninspired four-miler today. I wanted to stop at two miles. I again wanted to stop at three miles. I am proud of myself for reaching four miles.

***

There have been many meetings that monopolize my days. The advent of remote meetings via computer has increased the number of meetings among administrators.

Years ago, I learned an important lesson regarding meetings, that is, they are often used as a way to escape actually working. If a person is in a meeting, it is assumed that he or she is involved in something important. Unfortunately, and far too often, that isn't the case.

After years away from being able to interact in classrooms, I long to spend more time with the students and teachers as I used to. I would read to the kids, teach lessons sometimes, celebrate their birthdays, and always be around. It was great. That part of my job, which has always been the best part, has gone away, and I miss it greatly.

Wednesday, March 30, 2022
　　Day 89 – 4.1 miles

I ran FAST today, lightning fast today, completing four miles in 33:01. I wanted to break thirty-three minutes and came up just short. Still, it was my fastest four-miler of the year.

***

Yesterday a second grader made my day by sending me a Power Point with two slides.

The first slide read, "100% the best school."

The next slide read, "0% the worst school."

Thursday, March 31, 2022
　　Day 90 – 4.1 miles

I have now completed three months of daily running. 25% of the task is finished. I have a long way to go, but this was another huge step forward.

APRIL

"Nothing gold can stay."
Robert Frost

Friday, April 1, 2022
Day 91 – 4.1 miles

This morning I resolved to run faster than ever. And I did just that breaking 33-minutes for a four-miler.

So much of running is mental. The physical parts are real, but it's the mental part that makes the difference in achieving our goals or falling short of them.

Mind over matter is actually very true. There are times when the body is able to do more than we think possible. I know that when I have a positive mindset, I run my best.

Even with all the miles and races I have run, there are times when I lack confidence. On a day-to-day basis, as I start my runs, and often as I am running, I have doubts. I wonder if I am going to be strong enough to attain my goals.

This is one reason, I believe, I am trying to run every single day. I need to prove to myself that I have the physical and mental strength to push far beyond all limits and distractions to attain this goal.

When I was growing up, I was one of the youngest students in the grade. I was also the smallest. People always assumed I was weak. And, physically, as compared to the other students, I was. There is a part of me, as much as I might not want to admit it, that is still fighting those perceptions in my own mind. I have resolved throughout my life to be strong. Running each day for a year is one way I can prove that to myself.

In moments of weakness, we look at the struggles we are going through. In moments of strength, we see where we're going.

When we run, we find out who we are. Through the process, we can also create new narratives about ourselves.

Saturday, April 2, 2022
   Day 92 – 3.1 miles + 2.10 miles

With two runs today, I was finally able to reach 30 miles this week. My goal now is to build upon this progress, but that is not what has been on my mind.

***

There is a standard interview question that is asked when people first apply or interview for a job: "Where do you see yourself in five years?"

People don't ask, "Where do you see yourself in thirty-two years?"

In my profession, I achieved all the goals I set out to accomplish. I sustained and built up the most remarkable school anywhere. Over the last few years, I guided my school through the most challenging period in its history. It has all been great and wonderful and extremely rewarding.

But I know that it is time for me to step down and pass the torch to the next person who will help bring the school to even greater heights. I have my legacy. It is now time for a new person to come in and start to forge their own.

This month, I have to make my ultimate decision regarding retirement. It's one of the biggest steps I'll be taking in my life—a great leap into the vast unknown.

Sunday, April 3, 2022
    Day 93 – 2.1 miles

Alex, in Cambridge, Massachusetts, celebrates his 26th birthday today. I always feel empty when one of my sons has a birthday and I'm not there to celebrate the day with him.

***

I have been talking with my family, including my parents who were teachers for decades, for a long time about the next steps in my life. We have discussed all aspects of retirement and what comes next. There is a big difference, though, between talking about retiring and actually going through with it. I'm at the stage now where I have to act on this life-changing plan. They are all in support of me retiring.

Last night I talked with Ethan (who is wise beyond his years) about making my retirement official. Of all my children, Ethan has been the one who most closely saw and was part of my life as the principal of an elementary school.

Ethan was in fourth grade when I started at my school. He attended many school functions. Even today, he plays on a baseball team with me comprised mostly of fathers from my school community. Ethan has also worked in my school many times, helping me over breaks with any number of tasks including cleaning out closets and moving classroom furniture (again and again). As a college student on remote learning, and now as a college graduate, he's been a front seat observer to my life as a principal these last few years.

Ethan knows the school, the people, and the community. He knows why I love it all so much.

He has also seen how much has changed in recent years (and this does not imply that change is bad). Ethan's advice was straight forward. "Retire. Absolutely," he said.

I know I'll be making the right choice, but that does not make any of this easy.

***

I didn't get my run in today until the evening. The run was uninspired and short just to get it in. My mind is consumed with things other than running right now.

Monday, April 4, 2022
Day 94 – 5.4 miles

I rarely take days off from work, but needing some time, I took today off to finalize my decision to retire.

Retirement for me will be different than it is for many. I will be closing one door, but opening many others. I don't plan on slowing down. In fact, there is a great deal I need to accomplish in so many areas. Being retired will provide me more time to pursue those other interests and opportunities. I have more books to write, some requiring research that I cannot do at home and I'll need to travel for. I need to spend more time with my parents. I want to travel to all sorts of places with Laurie. On and on… One thing is for certain, I won't be sitting on a couch doing nothing.

***

It was a damp and chilly 50 degrees outside today, but I resolved to get out of the house for my run. I was hoping to push myself through a six-mile effort, and I came close. I ran the first three miles, but then walked and ran the final miles.

I'm not often pleased with myself when I have cut a run short and start walking, but today I didn't mind because my mind was heavy, and I appreciated the time alone and out of the house.

Tuesday, April 5, 2022
Day 95 – 2.1 miles

I cut off my run today at two miles. I was doing fine and running at an even pace. I felt good. Except... even with my decision to retire made up, even though I have known this is the right thing to do in my heart for a long time, the reality of it all is hitting me more than I thought it would.

It's very difficult to run with a heavy heart.

Wednesday. April 6, 2022
Day 96 – 4.1 miles

So much of running, as I continually learn, is mental. When my mind is light, my body feels the same way. When my mind is heavy, my runs are more sluggish.

My mind is lighter today because I met with my superintendent who provided the final clarity I needed to solidify my decision-making process.

He said, "You are in a great place. You had a great career. There's no need to do one more year."

We talked of life and goals and our futures. He is leaving our district for greener pastures and new opportunities. A new start. Me too.

I was touched, almost to tears, when he got up and hugged me as I left his office.

Thursday, April 7, 2022
Day 97 – 3.1 miles

I keep wanting to reach six miles, but I keep failing to get there. When I need to dig deep, I simply don't have any more to give. I am very disappointed in myself.

***

It's an emotional roller coaster in my head. Happy. Sad. Confident. Unsure.

Yesterday afternoon, as I sat through a never-ending meeting with a bunch of administrators all saying what could be done, what might be done, and what should be done, without every saying, "Let's get it done," I felt relief that I will never have to sit through meetings like that ever again.

Friday, April 8, 2022
Day 98 – 2.1 miles

Today as I finished my run, I was thinking about another player who went out on top...

It was the bottom of the eighth inning. The score was 4-1. Joe DiMaggio came to bat and connected for a double to right-center field. One half inning later, a pinch-hitter for the New York Giants, a lesser-known player named Sal Yvars, flew out to right field ending the 1951 World Series. DiMaggio and the Yankees were World Champions!

With that win Joe DiMaggio's career came to an end. He never played again. He retired a winner.

Saturday, April 9, 2022
Day 99 – 5.1 miles

I ran great today. With this being the first day of a ten-day school break, maybe that's all I needed.

Sunday, April 10, 2022
Day 100 – 4.1 miles

To celebrate my one hundredth consecutive day of running this year,

I ran a fast four miles on the treadmill. I never allowed the machine to get under 7.0 miles-per-hour. I appreciated the strenuousness of the exercise. I pushed myself, hard, feeling years younger. This is how I used to run. I rarely had easy days. If I was going to run, I was going to run hard.

Monday, April 11, 2022
Day 101 – 4.1 miles

Laurie and I are at the New Jersey shore to get away alone for a few days. My in-laws have a beach house that serves as a place of respite for us. It's nice to wake up at the beach.

I felt great on my run today. There are no hills here. I thought it would feel colder than the high 40's that it is, but it actually felt warmer. I thought I might run two slow miles, but instead I ran four. Sometimes a runner finds a groove and things seem to flow. I never doubted myself today, never felt the desire to stop. For a runner who doubts himself much more than he should, I see this as a huge step in the right direction.

Tuesday April 12, 2022
Day 102 – 3.0 miles

It is a cold, drizzly, and damp day at the Jersey shore. If I was home, I would be on the treadmill, but I don't have that luxury today. My run was nothing more than a task that had to be completed. It wasn't miserable, but it wasn't fun either.

Wednesday, April 13, 2022
Day 103 – 5.1 miles

Today, back home on the treadmill, I ran my fastest five-miler yet.

The students and teachers are still on spring break, but I'll be in my office at school today and tomorrow. Principals work over holidays and breaks. One thing I will really miss is my office at school where I can get things accomplished quietly in the empty building.

Thursday, April 14, 2022
Day 104 – 3.1 miles

The struggle with this quest to run every day is that there is always tomorrow to think about. The task is relentless. I wanted to push harder today, distance-wise, not with speed, but I only managed three miles before I stopped.

I feel successful because I ran, but I feel like I failed because I didn't run far enough.

Friday, April 15, 2022
Day 105 – 5.0 miles

I believe that today, Good Friday, the day that Christ died on the cross, is the holiest day of the year. I try to spend much time on Good Friday remembering the ultimate sacrifice Jesus made for us.

Last night, as I have done often, I played the role of Jesus at our church's reenactment of the Last Supper. It isn't too often that a bald guy without a beard plays the role of Christ, but I'm told that I do a good job. The whole experience is very meaningful to me.

***

Today was a beautiful spring day so I ran outside. I am looking forward to spring and summer when I'll be outside more often than not. I expected to have been outside a lot more than I have this year.

Saturday, April 16, 2022
Day 106 – 4.1 miles

Today I set out to do my fastest four-miler yet. And I succeeded.

Sunday, April 17, 2022
Day 107 – 4.9 miles

I was up early and I walked to church for the Easter Sunrise worship. Our church is about a mile-and-a-half from home. The temperature was still only in the 30's. Winter will not let up.

At the service, we sang the hymn, *Because He Lives*. The lyrics resonated with me, knowing that I can face tomorrow and all my fear is gone, because Jesus lives in me.

Tomorrow is when I will announce to my staff that this is my last year.

After breakfast, since they were home for Easter, Ryan, Tiffany, and I braved the chilly air and cool wind and covered 4.9 miles on a run around Wyckoff as we showed Tiffany some places that were meaningful in Ryan's life as he grew up. I loved having running buddies with me. This has been a singular pursuit, which sometimes gets pretty lonely.

Running is more wonderful when I share the miles with my family.

Monday, April 18, 2022
Day 108 – 3.1 miles

I never thought I could cry so loudly so silently.

Last night I went on the stationary bike, and rode for 30-minutes while listening to songs about saying goodbye. The tears just poured down my face. I hadn't cried like that in years. I didn't want my family to hear me so I cried in silence.

After the ride, I went into the hot tub alone into the dark outside where I contemplated all that lay ahead of me. I thought about the past and I considered what I hope my future holds.

Telling my staff of my coming retirement is going to be one of the most difficult things I have ever done. I have thought about what I am going to say a million different ways and I just don't know how it say it all.

I don't know how to say that I'm going to say goodbye.

***

Before work, I did three miles on the treadmill knowing, as I ran in place actually going nowhere, that I would soon be running directly into my brand-new future.

After today, nothing will ever be the same.

Tuesday, April 19, 2022
Day 109 – 3.1 miles

Yesterday's Faculty Meeting didn't go as planned, partially because I was never able to craft a very good plan.

As I thought about telling my staff that I'm going to retire, I kept picturing myself crying my eyes out in front of them. I worked myself up to be strong, and when I told them, they were stunned into silence. In my thoughts about that moment, I had come up with a million different things to say, but in the moment, me, a man of too many words, had none.

I simply told the staff that I was retiring and the room went silent. I filled the silence by telling them how much I loved them, but I wasn't all that articulate.

I finally said, "If I keep talking, I'll cry, and I don't want to do that... so I'll go now."

They clapped as I left the room. I was told that after I had departed, amid the shock, one teacher said aloud, "We're f***ed."

Over the next hour or so, the teachers came to my office to hug me, cry with me, and thank me. Many told me that I was the greatest boss they ever had. I then reached out to the presidents of the Home and School Association to ask them come to the school so I could tell them in person.

More sadness...

***

I'm sure some people feel I'm letting them down. I'm not a quitter, but I feel like one.

Every fighter thinks he has one last good fight in him. I know I don't.

***

At home, my family all stepped-up to give me support and love. Alex, who is still home for Easter, and Ethan brought a pizza home.

Ryan called to see how I was. My parents and in-laws too.

I also received a ton of loving e-mails and texts from my staff:

"Simply put, you are the GOAT! The Coach K of principals."

"You are so excellent at what you do. You've always known what matters ultimately - kindness and friendships. Your presence made

our school a truly special and magical place."

"Our school has grown exponentially under your leadership."

"Congrats Paul. You are and will always be the ideal Principal."
***

Full of emotions, sad and relieved, confident and frightened, secure and weak, I did three miles on the TM today.

I am usually able to absent my emotions when I run and just focus on that task. Running is often an escape. But right now, I have too many emotions and I cannot push them all aside. I carried all these feelings with me the entire way.

In another example of how life moves ever forward, I have an author visit at the Ramsey, New Jersey library tonight.

Wednesday, April 20, 2022
    Day 110 – 3.1 miles

I now live with this idea that I am ending my professional life.

The big question now becomes, "Who Am I?"
***

I am surprised that I have been able to keep up my running this week. If there ever was a week to quit, this has been it.

I thought I was done crying, or at least hoped I was, but I cried my way through the final miles of another run this morning. Three miles might be the best I can do for a while, and in a very real sense, getting that far is quite an accomplishment right now.

Thursday, April 21, 2022
    Day 111 – 3.1 miles

In his last at bat, ever, as a Yankee in Yankee Stadium, Derek Jeter lined a game-winning single to right field.

The Yankees didn't win the World Series that year, nor did they make the playoffs, but Jeter cemented his legacy by coming through in his final time at the plate.

I am looking to go out while I'm still at my best. I cannot imagine staying in my position and having people saying, "Dr. Sem, he used to be great, but he isn't any longer." That would kill me.

Friday, April 22, 2022
    Day 112 – 3.0 miles

When I shift from the treadmill to running on the roads, my feet often hurt. When I was younger, this did not happen as often, but now as I am older, I notice that it takes my body some time to acclimate to the hard roads.

Today I ran to my parents' house where we met to celebrate their 60th Wedding Anniversary. With retirement, I'll be able to see them a lot more often. That is a good and necessary thing.

Saturday, April 23, 2022
    Day 113 – 4.1 miles

I had to get my run in early today as Ethan and I are going to the Yankees game later with a bunch of families from my school. They keep telling me not to retire.

Sunday, April 24, 2022
    Day 114 – 3.0 miles

Ethan and I had a baseball game this morning, as we do most Sundays. I love playing ball with him. I didn't pitch today, and instead played some second base and centerfield. At bat, I struck out and walked. I then stole second base. As a pitcher, I don't bat very often, and I also do not get many hits. This was my first stolen base since I was in high school.

I ran after the game, but didn't venture too far from my house because my stomach was a little queasy.

Monday, April 25, 2022
Day 115 – 4.1 miles

Time is a great elixir. With time comes peace. Contentment. As I slowly get beyond the raw emotions that came from announcing my retirement, I am starting to feel like my old self again. Even though everything in my life is changing drastically, I am, ironically, starting to feel that my life is returning to normal.

Feeling like I had a little more in me than I have had in recent weeks, I set out today to run my fastest four-miler of the year and finished at 32:24. Feeling very proud of myself, I couldn't wait to record my run on my workout calendar. It turns out that this was not my fastest run of 2022. About nine days ago I ran this distance in 32:11.

I don't even remember that run.

***

Tonight, I am being recognized at the Board of Education meeting as they express gratitude for my years of service to the district.

Tuesday, April 26, 2022
Day 116 – 3.1 miles + 3.1 miles

Perfunctory. Or that's what I thought.

Last night the Ridgewood Board of Education recognized me as they accepted (with regret) my retirement. I figured there would be a nice moment, a few words from the superintendent, and then I'd be on my way. Laurie attended the meeting with me. I told her not to expect anything grand.

I was surprised to see teachers, parents, and students attending. There had to be fifty people there for me. After the superintendent spoke, the crowd gave me a standing ovation.

As part of the meeting, a number of parents gave speeches and paid tribute to me. I didn't expect any of that to happen.

This was anything but perfunctory and my heart is forever touched.

***

I didn't sleep all that well last night and was up for good a little after 3:00 a.m. I keep telling myself that I'm fine. I might be. I'm not really sure how I feel. My emotions are all over the place. To kill some time, I rode the exercise bike at 4:15 a.m. for 20 minutes.

I then got my run in which was impressive considering the fact that I was half asleep when I ran.

On my way to work, to try to wake up a bit, I drank a can of Dr. Pepper. The bellyache that followed wasn't fun.

***

In the evening, I felt the need to get an additional run in. I like "double days" (and not just because, as a baseball fan I like saying "Doubleday"). I feel that running twice in a day helps me gain more strength, more power, and more energy.

I believe that this is also a great way to accumulate miles when I have less time for a long run. As I understand the research, two five-mile runs in one day are just as beneficial to one's endurance as one ten-mile run. As I grow older, I am finding that these double days help me reach some necessary mileage in my marathon training plans.

Wednesday, April 27, 2022
    Day 117 – 3.1 miles

I am close to completing my fourth month and I am somewhat surprised that my body has not broken down or even shown signs of breaking down. I'm used to having my back flare up. That happens to me on occasion like it did in February. I've lived with that my whole life. I also have a chiropractor and a son who is a chiropractor who have always been able to fix me when I find myself in pain. What is surprising is that I haven't felt knee pain or true soreness in my quads or thighs. The daily running is not breaking my body down.

Years ago, I read all sorts of research that demonstrated that running is not bad for one's knees as so many say. I believe (without any scientific proof, just myself) that daily vigorous exercise helps the body rather than hurts it.

One would think that with all this exercise, I'd be tired much more often, but instead it provides me with energy.

Thursday, April 28, 2022
    Day 118 – 4.1 miles

Last night I had another book talk, this one at my "home" library in Wyckoff. A grand total of three people showed up. Three. It's not easy being a world-famous author who no one has heard of or who comes out to listen to.

Friday, April 29, 2022
    Day 119 – 2.1 miles

There is an old quote that is out there that reads, *"It's not the run, it's the runner."* This is absolutely true. Sometimes I get so focused on the miles or the time or the effort (or all of the above) that I lose sight of the fact that the main thing in this sport is just getting out there and getting it done.

In the end, the effort is all that matters. It's all that should matter. The other stuff is just window dressing. As long as I am moving, I am achieving.

Today all I did was get it done – minimally. Since I was working on only four hours of sleep after a late baseball game last night, I didn't have much in me.

Still, I kept the streak alive. I kept moving. It wasn't the run. That didn't matter. What mattered was the runner. Me. I got it done. I am most proud of myself when I run on the days when I most don't think I can.

Saturday, April 30, 2022
Day 120 – 4.1 miles

Laurie and I returned to the beach last night for the weekend, so I was able to get outside to run where the roads are nice and quiet and flat. I am one-third of the way through my quest. I am very confident right now that I will make it.

MAY

"You are tomorrow what you believe today."
Gary Elliott

Sunday, May 1, 2022
Day 121 – 6.2 miles

I have found that oftentimes the most difficult mile in a 5K (3.1 mile) race is the second one. There is some comfort in knowing that the first mile is over, but there are still two-thirds of the race to go. What often lies ahead is pain and a great deal of effort. I feel like that today. I finished the first third of my 365-day journey. Now comes what might be the most challenging part, the middle third.

***

Today I ran a strong 6.2 miles on one of my favorite courses at the beach. Much of this run is on the boardwalk in Lavalette, New Jersey. It always feels like summer when I'm running there.

When he was younger, my father-in-law used to accompany me on my runs at the beach. He'd ride a bicycle and I'd run. I always ran a little faster when he was with me. I never wanted any runner to pass me as we traversed the miles on the boardwalk and for the most part, no one ever did!

I haven't had a long run like this in weeks. I call a run like today's a "confidence builder."

Monday, May 2, 2022
Day 122 – 3.1 miles

Since we're on a school holiday today, I spent most of the day on an initial review of this manuscript. Writing is a lot like running. It's a daily process and one only gets better through practice and repetition. I have become a better runner because I have invested great amounts of time into running. The same is true for my writing.

When we fully invest in a process, positive results come – maybe not immediately, but certainly over time.

Tuesday, May 3, 2022
Day 123 – 5.1 miles

I pushed hard today to get my first five-miler on the treadmill in quite some time. I wanted to cover the distance and do it in under 9-minute miles. I succeeded, but it was a struggle throughout. The struggle, though, is good news for me. I am finding that I can, once again, dig a little deeper to accomplish my goals. For weeks, I did not have the inner strength necessary to get through the difficult parts of my runs.

Now that I have come to grips with the reality that I am retiring, I'm feeling a bit more at ease. This newly found contentment is showing in my recent runs.

Wednesday, May 4, 2022
Day 124 – 4.1 miles

And then, all of a sudden, my right calf has been tight. It doesn't hurt, necessarily, but it is sore. This probably comes from too many long or faster runs. Sometimes if I push too hard, I injure myself. Finding that necessary balance has always been a struggle for me. I have often thought that it showed weakness if I stopped running or took too many days off because of pain. This is probably one reason I had tears in my Achilles tendon.

Finding the correct balance this year, while running every single day, has been a particular struggle. Today I ran on the treadmill, keeping the speed, at 6.1 and covering the miles slowly. I am constantly re-minding myself that if I push too hard and get injured, I'll fail in my attempt to run every day. If I fail, I'll have no other choice but to try again next year.

I am tired of thinking about this goal and wondering if I can do it. I have to make it work and get it done this year.

Thursday, May 5, 2022
Day 125 – 3.1 miles

The right calf is still tight. I did some work on it with my Hypervolt (a powerful hand-held massage tool) before my run today.

I also went to PT yesterday, but I had my right arm worked on rather than my legs. I hope to pitch tonight. My arm, that started hurting in late March, still isn't totally better and I'm not going to miss a chance to pitch. I never want to let pain get in the way of competing.

***

A few weeks ago, there was a bomb threat at some local schools including the high school in our district. There are a million reasons why I am retiring. The burden of keeping everyone safe in a world where school violence seems to happen so often is one big reason. I think about the safety of the students and teachers throughout every single day. It's a huge responsibility to shoulder.

Friday, May 6, 2022
Day 126 – 4.1 miles

I pitched last night and did great. I went six innings allowing only two runs. I struck out four. We won 11-2.

So much of running, so much of life itself, centers on how we deal with the events and circumstances that impact our daily lives. I'm feeling less stress and more content. As a result, my physical perfor-mances have been improving.

Saturday, May 7, 2022
    Day 127 – 3.1 miles + 2.0 miles

I am frustrated because I seem stuck on the treadmill. I want to run outside, but the weather is miserable. It's pouring rain. It's also still only in the 40's. This has been the coldest spring I ever remember. The warm weather just won't come and stay.

***

I was reflecting about a running experience I had on a cruise. One morning as I was getting some miles on the ship's jogging track, a somewhat obnoxious runner sprinted past me a few times. He was lapping me and was acting quite smug about his running skills. He carried a definite "I am better than you" aura about himself as he zoomed past me time and again.

A few days later, I was on one of the treadmills in the fitness center. I was a few miles into my workout. Even though there were a host of empty machines in the gym, he chose the one right next to me and started to run, very fast, again. I determined in that moment to outlast this guy. No matter how long he ran, I was going to run longer. I was a few weeks into training for a marathon so I knew I could outlast him. Even if I couldn't, I would have anyway.

He kept running, but so did I.

Eventually, he quit. I didn't stop until he had long since left the area.

Sunday, May 8, 2022
    Day 128 – 4.0 miles

It's Mothers' Day and Ryan and Tiffany will come out for the day. Because of a family party, I won't be able to make time to run with them. I needed to get my run in early, and even though it was chilly, I ran outside. I need to get off that treadmill, but, like a magnet, it seems to call me to it.

Last night, at about 8:00 p.m., I jumped on the treadmill to do two extra miles. I did these purposefully slow so I could reach 30 miles for the week.

Monday, May 9, 2022
   Day 129 – 5.1 miles

There is a huge difference between wanting something to happen and working hard to make it happen. Success does not come to those who just wish and hope. Success comes to those who work for it.

Often people seek to find the easy solutions to any number of challenges. Fitness is one great example of this. There is a plethora of advertisements for products that'll supposedly allow people to lose weight effortlessly.

It just doesn't work that way. To lose weight and get stronger, one has to eat right and exercise.

For the changes to become permanent, these behaviors must also become habits. They need to become part of one's daily life.

Too often people look to tomorrow as the time when they'll start anew. The problem is that most often those tomorrows never come.

The better tact is to seek to achieve the goals today. Right now. I made a decision, decades ago to give my health and fitness my best efforts. I started, I committed, and I am continuing. I want to be vibrant and in great health in my old years.

Who knows, maybe I'll run a marathon when I'm eighty-years-old. Maybe at ninety too!

Tuesday, May 10, 2022
   Day 130 – 4.1 miles

I know that good results do not happen unless we work for them. We can't simply wish for things to take care of themselves.

I have been wishing for my sugar numbers to come down. I have been over 100 on my daily morning checks for weeks. I then snack on sugary sweets and drink soda during the day and hope that when I awake, my numbers will magically be better.

Yesterday, I finally got my glucose under 100. I took a huge sigh of relief when the monitor registered 95. I then started eating M&M's and today it was back over 100. I'm frightened that one day I'll be a diabetic.

I need to get more self-discipline, in regard to my eating habits or I will be.

Wednesday, May 11, 2022
Day 131 – 4.1 miles

I'm getting close to the point where my marathon training will begin. As this period approaches, I start to feel a very real change in myself. I'm not necessarily anxious or nervous, but I think more and more of the big race and the long training necessary in order to get there. I have been doing great with my daily runs. I am not surprised that I have maintained the focus to get this far, deep down I know I can do this, but I am surprised, even disappointed in myself, that I have not been running longer distances. In a perfect world, I would have had a few ten-mile runs under my belt by now. I need to build a strong base because the long runs, the fifteen to twenty-milers, frighten me. I dread the long runs.

Thursday, May 12, 2022
Day 132 – 5.1 miles

Today will be one of those days when I won't get any rest.

After work, I'll wrap things up in my office and head into the town to scoop ice cream at Ben & Jerry's for a school fund raiser. I'll then rush to my baseball game in the next town. I'm the starting pitcher tonight.

***

My favorite memory from an ice cream scooper night occurred about eight years ago. I wore a button-down dress shirt, right from work, into Ben & Jerry's and then scooped for three hours. I remember that day being extremely warm.

As I scooped, I got tons of ice cream, mostly dark chocolate flavors, all over my shirt. I was a mess. When my shift ended, I rushed out because I wanted to see Ethan in his school play that night.

I went directly from ice cream scooping to Ethan's high school a few towns away. The play had already started, and Ethan's big lines were in the first act so I had no time to stop home and change my clothes.

As I entered the building, people started looking at me with very concerned expressions. I looked down at my shirt, covered with dark marks embedded into the fabric. The stains looked less like chocolate ice cream and more like blood. My tie was askew. I probably looked like an axe murderer who had just performed some horrible act.

I kept saying, to anyone who would listen, "It's dried ice cream... I was at a fund raiser for my school. I had to rush to get here..."

I'm pretty certain some of the people who saw me that night haven't talked to me since.

Friday, May 13, 2022
   Day 133 – 2.1 miles

I don't like to admit this, but today, I am exhausted. Wiped out.

Scooping was great. Baseball wasn't. We lost. We got crushed. My arm kills.

I consider two-mile runs almost cheating. It doesn't take much of an effort at this point for me to slog along on the treadmill for twenty minutes to simply cover two meaningless miles. But, I didn't have anything else in me today.

Saturday, May 14, 2022
    Day 134 – 6.1 miles

I didn't get my run in until 8:15 p.m. today because we had a garage sale which can be an exhausting experience.

I jumped on the TM knowing I needed six miles to reach 30 miles for the week, but I had fallen asleep watching the Yankees. Bleary-eyed, I started running and didn't stop until I reached my goal. It's not like me, but I didn't look at my stop time when I finished.

I was just glad it was over.

Sunday, May 15, 2022
    Day 135 – 4.0 miles

It rained all morning cancelling our baseball game, but by the early afternoon it stopped raining, and I was able to get outside, where I really long to be, for my run.

***

There have been a number of technological advances that have helped me as a runner in various ways. My GPS watch is one of them.

When I first started running, I would drive my running routes in my car to determine just how far each was. I then followed those exact routes precisely, so I'd always know the distances I ran. I am a slave to keeping an accurate accounting of my runs.

Years later, on-line programs like *Map My Run* began to allow runners to plot their runs on a map to calculate the distances of their efforts. I counted my miles using that program for decades, but about a year ago, I got a Garmin GPS watch, and it has changed everything for me. This technology has literally opened up the world. I can now run anywhere and know exactly how far I have gone and how long it has taken me. I can even monitor my pace as I go. I am no longer a slave to the routes I mapped out. The GPS watch provides the technology of a treadmill on my wrist. All of this liberates me. I have lived in this area for most of my life, but I'm now running on roads and paths I've never been on before.

Monday, May 16, 2022

Day 136 – 2.1 miles + 2.1 miles

After my run yesterday, I met with Roy White to continue the work on our book.

When I was a kid, I became a Yankees fan, in large part, because our twin neighbors, who lived across the street, were Yankees fans. Their favorite player was Roy White. One of the twins, now approaching 60-years-old, has colon cancer.

When I was with Roy White, I broke the rule I established for myself and asked for his autograph on a get-well card for my former neighbor. Roy White, of course, signed the card.

Life is better when we give of our abundance for others.

***

Last night our doorbell rang at about 1:15 a.m. Some kids in the neighborhood thought it would be fun to ring people's doorbells in the middle of the night. It wasn't fun for me.

I never got back to sleep and had only two miles in me this morning. I tried to make up the difference with another two miles on the TM before bed.

Tuesday, May 17, 2022
   Day 137 – 3.1 miles

I'm battling a cold. As the day progressed yesterday, I started losing my voice. I put my "home remedy" theory into practice and ran hard to try to sweat it out of my system.

I can't afford to get sick. There are a ton of events at school coming up including running our Kindergarten Orientation programs, hosting a special breakfast with some students, working with my Principal for the Day, and then the school play is this weekend. I have never been the type to take days off and I don't plan to start doing that now. I cannot allow myself to get sick.

Wednesday, May 18, 2022
   Day 138 – 4.1 miles

Yesterday I bought bagels and fruit for a special "Breakfast with Dr. Sem" that I hosted for some students whose parents won this as a prize at a school event. I bring whatever food the children (or their parents) request. This year I was asked to provide fruit and bagels.

The kids arrived and started commenting immediately:

"I don't want a bagel," said one.

"I don't like fruit," said another.

When it was over, I threw away five partially eaten bagels and left a big tray of fruit for the teachers as a result of the special "Let's Not Eat Breakfast with Dr. Sem."

Thursday, May 19, 2022
   Day 139 – 4.1 miles

There are some events that are difficult to explain even after they occur...

Yesterday, as I worked with a third-grade student who was the Principal for the Day, former Yankee Darryl Strawberry, the great baseball player, walked into my office.

I sat with my mouth agape thinking, "Darryl Strawberry...is here? Why is Darryl Strawberry here?"

He came over to me and shook my hand. We took a picture together... and then things started to move very quickly.

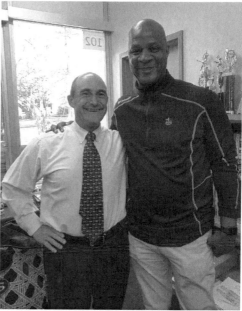

My secretary came in with a bag Laurie had sent in with some Yankees shirts, but more importantly, my baseball glove. Someone said that Darryl wanted to have a catch with me.

"You want to have a catch?" I asked.

An announcement was then made on the school's PA system, "Students please head outside to the baseball field to watch Dr. Sem have a catch with Darryl Strawberry."

Never in my life have I ever had a catch with a professional baseball player, but there we were, on the school's baseball field, with all of the students and the teachers watching. Darryl Strawberry and I were tossing a baseball back-and-forth. Soon everyone came onto the field to take a photo with Darryl and me.

We then went back inside and talked briefly. Darryl Strawberry kept saying to me, "This is for you. This is all for you." He thanked me, time and again, for being such a great school leader.

In total, he must have stayed for 45 minutes. When he left, I gave him a hug and said, "I love you, Darryl." And he said, "I love you too."

Friday, May 20, 2022
Day 140 – 3.1 miles

Darryl Strawberry had some difficult personal struggles in his life, but then he found God—or as he tells the story, God found him.

Life isn't easy. It's not easy for teachers or principals or even Major League Baseball players. We all make mistakes. We have all done things we are not proud of. One of the lessons I have always taught the students is that it is important to own our mistakes and find ways to fix them, or at the very least to apologize. To me the words, "I'm sorry" mean "it won't happen again." In my own life, seeking God's forgiveness for my mistakes is something I ask for. It's all right there in *The Lord's Prayer*. I'm reminded of this with the prayers I recite every mile I run.

One of the teachers gave me a book Darryl Strawberry recently wrote about his faith journey. I look forward to reading it.

Saturday, May 21, 2022
Day 141 – 3.6 miles

People complain when the weather gets hot outside, but I enjoy it. Today was the first day over 90 degrees. I wait all winter for days like this.

I thought about pushing the distance and running far, but at three miles the heat actually caught up to me. I walked for a moment or two before running the final 6/10th of a mile home.

With 26.2 miles for the week, I fell short of thirty miles, but that's okay. I'm quite happy with the distance I managed overall. I'm a big fan of 26.2 miles.

Sunday, May 22, 2022
  Day 142 – 3.0 miles

This morning Ethan and I played baseball. I was the starting pitcher and pitched one of my best games. I went five innings, struck out five, including three in one inning, and gave up just one run. We won.

Then I met with Roy White to continue our work before I had a chance in the late afternoon to get my run in.

It was again very hot, which I tend to enjoy, but I was tired and was not going to push it. I resolved to cover three or four easy miles doing my best to avoid as many of the hills as possible. As I reached the three-mile mark, my parents happened to drive by, and they offered to take me home.

I don't like to take the easy way out but took them up on their offer.

Monday, May 23, 2022
  Day 143 – 4.1 miles

Today begins a four-day work week. We'll be off on Friday to begin a long Memorial Day weekend.

I did four miles on the TM. Over the last week, once again, I have not been listening to music when I run. It's better for my ears that way. I actually wish I could run like this every day, but I actually love the loud songs as I run. It's a bad habit and is probably self-destructive.

After school today, I'm taking some fourth graders bowling as another of the prizes I gave out a few weeks ago. Right now, families win charity auctions to have their children spend time with me. Soon, no one will even care who I am.

Tuesday, May 24, 2022
  Day 144 – 6.1 miles

This morning I ran hard on the treadmill. I was strong and focused, and I was able to concentrate on the run, in doing what was necessary. Throughout, I simply embraced the sport of running. I focused on being active, and alive—and on the physical endeavor itself. I didn't let any other thoughts get in my way.

Success comes from the ability to focus on being one's best in the task at hand.

Wednesday, May 25, 2022
Day 145 – 3.2 miles + 3.3 miles

Yesterday in Texas there was another school shooting. I can't watch any of the television coverage. I can't imagine the horror and devastation the people are all living through.

I wish we, as a society, would just take the time to truly love and respect one another. No hate. No name calling. Just love.

If we were taught to love each other, just as the Bible says, to truly love each other, to care and respect and value each person as a unique and special individual, the world would be a better place.

***

Today was a "double-day" of runs, neither very long, but both outside. I don't particularly enjoy running outside before work. I have this irrational fear that I'll be late.

Thursday, May 26, 2022
Day 146 – 4.1 miles

About my fitness, I am still, in many regards, right where I was in January when I started this whole process of running every day. I am surprised that my running hasn't improved a great deal.

I would have imagined that by now, I would be routinely and easily cranking out longer and faster runs. Instead, I seem to be on a treadmill, literally and figuratively. I can't seem to get anywhere except to be right where I was when I started.

***

Today we're having a whole day celebration of music and the arts in school. There will be performances all over the campus all day long. Parents and grandparents and siblings (young and old) will be around to watch the students perform.

In a way, school will be a bit like Disney World today with happy kids, happy families, and lots of beautiful music.

Friday, May 27, 2022
   Day 147 – 4.2 miles

It's great to be loved. At the music and arts celebration yesterday, each fourth-grade class did a Reader's Theater production of my children's book *Principal Sam and the Three Bears*.

Later, the fifth-grade band did a rendition of the song *From A Wigwam* from the John Thompson book for beginning piano players. As a child, that was one of the only songs I ever learned how to play on the piano. My sister, who took piano lessons, taught it to me. Over the years, I have been known to interrupt instrumental music lessons by going to the piano in the classroom and playing that simple song. Our instrumental music teacher taught the children how to play it as a small tribute to me.

***

We're closed for a long Memorial Day weekend. I did a lot of writing this morning and then went outside for a nice and easy run.

I love the Garmin watch. With the GPS, I just run. I have lived in this area for most of my life. I live within two miles of my childhood home, but there are some streets I have never been on—places I have no reason to go. As I run, I am experiencing my hometown area in ways I've never done before.

***

Tomorrow is the Spring Lake Five Mile Run, my favorite non-NYC Marathon race in the world. I have run that race more than 25 times. The Spring Lake 5, to me, signals the beginning of summer. Alex will be home later today and he, Ethan, and I will run the race tomorrow. I suspect they'll both cover the distance a lot faster than me.

Saturday, May 28, 2022
   Day 148 – 5.0 miles

Here's the thing about running, and life—we can do more than we ever thought possible. This morning Alex, Ethan, and I ran the Spring Lake Five.

Knowing that most of my outside runs have been at about 9:30 pace, I was hoping to finish in about 47:30. I would have been pleased with that. But then something happened along the way...

The race started, and I went out strong. I wanted to run a good race (and I wanted to beat my sons), but I didn't push too hard. I went with the crowd, darting around the slower runners as best as I could in this race with about 9,000 participants.

As we reached the one-mile marker, the clock read 8:03.

All at once and doing some quick mental math, I realized that if I could run the next three miles at nine-minute-mile pace, and then run a ten-minute final mile, I'd finish at 45:00 minutes, way ahead of my goal. I told myself, "Do not be afraid to be great today."

The clock at the two-mile mark wasn't working, but at the third mile, I saw that I was still doing great. I was just over 24 minutes. I had run three miles at about eight-minute-mile pace. This was insane!

I kept telling myself the same message, "Don't be afraid to be great." I pushed hard for the final two miles and finished at 39:52.

I hadn't run that race that fast since 2015. I didn't think I had that kind of speed in me. I was faster than 91% of the other runners (including Alex and Ethan) in that race.

Today I had confidence and I performed well. So much of how we perform depends on our mindset.

Sunday, May 29, 2022
Day 149 – 3.0 miles

The whole family is at the beach for the weekend. These moments are very special, but fleeting. They never last long enough; the days go too quickly.

Ryan, Tiffany, and I ran three miles by going up and down all the various streets around the beach house. We did every road including the dead ends. The house is on a small island, one wouldn't think there were three miles of roads there.

Monday, May 30, 2022
Day 150 – 6.2 miles + 3.1 miles

Today seems like a big milestone in this running journey. 150 days is significant.

Every year on Memorial Day I wake up super early from the beach and drive home to participate in the Ridgewood Run. This is the annual road race in my school community, and I always participate. This will probably be my last Ridgewood Run. I promised my family that I wouldn't leave the beach early just to run for and with my school once I'm no longer the principal.

I don't know how I did it again, but I absolutely killed the 10K finishing in 50:04. I don't know where I found this speed. It was very hot on the course, with lots of hills, yet I was able to cover the miles quickly. Maybe, since it's my last Ridgewood Run ever, I wanted to try to show off a bit.

I ran the 5K a lot slower since I ran it with a third-grade student and his dad. The student had fun for much of the race, darting around to sprinklers and hoses, but the heat eventually got to him. He showed the best characteristic runners have, perseverance, by pushing through and finishing.

Before the race they mentioned my name on the PA a few times, "Congrats to Dr. Sem who is running his final Ridgewood Run as a principal in Ridgewood." When they first made this announcement, as we stood at the start, I almost cried. I never expected them to announce my name at the race.

Tuesday, May 31, 2022
   Day 151 – 3.1 miles

Those races yesterday, along with the sun and the heat, took a lot out of me. I wasn't myself yesterday afternoon. I was physically drained; my stomach was queasy. I spent a lot of time just sitting which is foreign to me.

I need to learn how to take it easy. I'm good at running hard. I'm good at working hard. I'm good at juggling a million different tasks.

I'm not good at relaxing. I don't know how to do it. I hope I don't have too much of it in retirement.

JUNE

"And, in the end, the love we take is equal to the love we make."
The Beatles

Wednesday, June 1, 2022
    Day 152 – 5.1 miles

Working on only four hours of sleep, I was an animal today. I jumped on the TM and ran five hard miles in 43:38.

I got home late last night after a baseball game and am still fired up. I was the starting pitcher and was a bulldog. I had a live fastball, and my curveball was on point. My catcher, our coach Rick, called a great game. I threw up and down, side to side, changing speeds, and had them guessing all game long. In the first inning, they had runners on second and third and only one out. I pitched out of that without giving up a run. I then threw four shutout innings. With a 6-0 lead, the other team scored three unearned runs off me in the sixth, but I got out of the inning and that was that. We won 11-4.

Still thriving from the positive adrenaline off my performance last night, my run today was also extremely strong and of the highest quality.

Logically, I should have had a difficult run today. I threw a lot of pitches last night. I didn't sleep well. I should be exhausted physically. But because my mind was still enthused and my confidence high, my run followed suit.

Running is as much a mental sport as a physical one. Good thoughts lead to good results.

Thursday, June 2, 2022
   Day 153 – 2.1 miles

By the time I got home yesterday after a long day at work with a million things that came up regarding students, inappropriate behaviors, angry parents, upset teachers, and more followed by our end-of-the-year party for the administrative team, I was shot. I had nothing in the tank. I was asleep by 7:00 p.m.

This morning, the alarm woke me at 4:00 a.m. I wanted to sleep more. I decided to do the smart thing and do a short and slow run rather than pushing myself any more than I have already this week. A body can only do so much.

As a general philosophy, I do not believe that "good enough actually is," but as I work through this process of running every day, I have learned that on occasion, good enough is, in reality... good enough. I am fearful of falling into the trap that always allows me to take the easy way out, but there are times when a person doesn't have anything more to give.

Friday, June 3, 2022
   Day 154 – 5.1 miles

Some mornings I wake up and I just know I "have it." Today I blasted through five miles on the treadmill.

When things go well, it's swell.

The art of running isn't how strong the body is. My body is obviously strong. It's how strong the mind is. The question isn't what our body can do, it's what our mind will allow us to do.

Saturday, June 4, 2022
   Day 155 – 3.1 miles

A long day, but a great day. I began the day with my weekly walk with Mike and Colin. Then came my Saturday podcast. Following that I attended a book festival as a featured author. I met some great people, sold a few books, and had a nice day.

Finally, at 8:45 p.m. I got on the TM for an easy three miles to wrap up another 30-mile week. I seem to be now reaching thirty-mile weeks routinely. I hope that I am getting ready to step up the milage.

Sunday, June 5, 2022
   Day 156 – 3.3 miles

At times I have surprised myself with the fact that I have made it this far running every day. It hasn't been easy. Each day the task looms over me. In the mornings, I am often tired. I think about the runs ahead with more than a little dread.

It takes a great deal of mental strength to know that one is about to willingly enter a period of physically suffering. I need to be clear about that. Running can be fun and invigorating, but it is also a difficult physical exercise. In every run there are aspects of pain and suffering. Sometimes the runner suffers more, but it's a truism that even easy runs aren't easy.

I am getting it done, but there have been days, like today, when I have not wanted to run. At all. I dreaded running before I went outside and hated every single step. I tried to pick a flat route, but nothing around here is totally flat and nothing interested me.

Today running was a chore.

Earlier in the day, we had a baseball game over an hour away. The game itself took five hours. I played left field and made an error. I made a base running blunder and was thrown out. In right field later in the game I caught a fly ball and fell down. I then pitched in relief in the 10th inning and blew the game. We lost. It was all on me.

It is no wonder I hated the run. My negative self-thoughts doomed my run before I even started.

Monday, June 6, 2022
    Day 157 – 3.2 miles

My goal, now that the school year is winding down and the weather is warm, is to run more outside. I hope to be away from the treadmill more often than not. I wait all year for the warm air. I plan to take advantage of it as often as I can.

When I'm running outside before work, I'm always afraid that I'll be late to work, yet I finished my run at 6:24 a.m. which is about 30 minutes ahead of when I get off the TM on most mornings.

Today I reached back and pushed my speed. I averaged 7:55 miles by running negative splits:
- Mile 1 = 8:28
- Mile 2 = 8:05
- Mile 3 = 7:29

***

I have some (hopefully final) stressful meetings at work this week. There are administrators outside my building who wish to make changes to a program at my school without any input from any stakeholders (meaning the teachers, the parents, or even the principal—me). What often happens in situations like this is that I have to go to great lengths to defend my school, its culture, the programs, the staff, and more. It seems that some of the people I deal with do not understand how excellent schools operate. I am tired of fighting battles like this.

I hope the school district will name a new principal soon so I can let that new person shadow me for a bit to get a sense of what the job, but more importantly, what my school, is all about. My school is different than any other, it is a place of joy and learning and creativity. It will behoove the new principal to get an understanding of the school culture to help assure his or her success.

I have been handling the emotions of seeing my long and successful career coming to a close pretty well, I think. I'm going to miss it all, but right now, I just want it to end. There's been a lot of garbage these last few years and it has taken a lot out of me. I wish that wasn't so. I know I don't have another year of battling people over the poor decisions they make that impact the students and the teachers and the school I am responsible for.

This doesn't mean I don't love my school or my job, it just means that I'm very tired and that I don't have much more to give. I realized this year that I don't have another year in me. I gave it everything I had, for more than three decades, but in doing so, it has left me somewhat empty. I also believe that change is good. I had my run. The school will thrive under a new leader. We're all replaceable. I know I am.

Tuesday, June 7, 2022
Day 158 – 4.2 miles

As I ran today, I thought a lot during my "mile prayers." There's a passage in The Lord's Prayer, that reads, *"And forgive us our trespasses as we forgive those who trespass against us."*

I often ask God to forgive my mistakes and to give me the strength and character to forgive others. I believe I am getting there, but this is very difficult to do. Forgiveness is difficult, especially when we think we've been wronged. It's important for us to understand that we are also, often, part of the problem and that we need others to also forgive us. The healing process works best when we focus less on the perceived slights against us, and we work to find ways to repair the wrongs we have done to others.

This morning was my third day in a row running outside in the early morning hours. I like this, a lot. When I run outside, there is no music blasting in my ears. It's quiet. It's nice. It's peaceful. I loved almost every step of my run today, which doesn't happen very often.

Wednesday, June 8, 2022
Day 159 – 4.2 miles

This morning I was out running with the early sunrise (about 5:15 a.m.) which filled me with awe. How beautiful the world can be when we take the time to notice it. Most often the sun rises while we're sleeping or taking part in other tasks around the home. How often does the sun rise while we are typing away on a keyboard or watching a silly video? The sunrise is a gift of majesty and splendor that goes unnoticed almost every day by most, myself included. I need to make more time to notice it. I believe my life will be enriched beyond measure if I take the time to seek and see more of the beauty in the world (and in the people) around me.

Without my phone (and music), it's just me and the roads and the scenery. I wear a ROAD-ID with my name, address, and phone number on it just in case I fall, or have a heart attack, or get run over. Who knows, maybe I will get attacked by a bear. More likely is that a dog will run from its yard and bite me. I have always been afraid of dogs.

There is a location where I often run that once brought me face to face with an animal. Years ago, in the early morning, a large deer hopped right past me. The deer had just crossed a highway and must have been frightened. As she went by, in an instant, I could have sworn she was a kangaroo. Ever since, my family has known that stretch of road as "Kangaroo Curve."

Thursday, June 9, 2022
Day 160 – 5.1 miles

In spite of the fact that it is a very rainy morning, I had considered going outside to run, but I lacked the courage and decided the treadmill was good enough.

Sometimes I find myself in a strange place emotionally because leaving my job for good frightens the heck out of me.

It also rained a lot last night so I don't know how the baseball field looks, but if it is dry by tonight, I'm pitching. I'm also pitching Sunday morning. This will be a huge test for my perpetually sore right arm.

Friday, June 10, 2022
Day 161 – 2.1 miles

My arm passed the first test with flying colors. We won 17-4. I went the distance (seven innings, since the mercy rule applied). Against one of the better hitting teams, I allowed a few runs early, but my team battled and then they put the game away.

What pleased me most about this game was the fact that I wasn't sharp. My fastball wasn't fast, my control was a bit off, and my curve ball didn't curve. I also couldn't see my catcher's signs very well so I wasn't even throwing (or trying to throw) what he asked for half the time. I gave up single runs in the first three innings and then didn't allow another run until the last inning, and that run came only after two errors. It was great, but I didn't get home until after midnight.

Today is the first of two Field Days at school. Today will be for grades three, four, and five. On Monday we'll do the program for the kindergarten, first, and second grades. Later this morning, as part of Field Day, I'll run the dance station leading the kids through Cotton Eye Joe, the Macarena, and the Cha Cha Slide. I have about two hours of dancing ahead of me. The kids seem to love it (and who am I kidding, I do too).

Saturday, June 11, 2022
   Day 162 – 3.1 miles

Dancing was a blast. I love when the kids leave my "dance party" saying, "That was the best!" Some adults said after, "There's no way the next principal will do that for the kids."

Then, after school, we had our annual school picnic, really a nice evening activity. Tons of current and former parents and students came to thank me for all I have done as the principal. I almost cried a few times, but I held it together.

***

Tomorrow is a special event for my retirement. They are having a "Walk-off for Dr. Sem" celebration at Yogi Berra Stadium. Ryan and Tiffany and Alex and Perri will come home today. Ethan will, of course, also be there.

With a lot planned, I had to get my run in early and went outside staying only around my neighborhood. My legs are heavy and sore after all the dancing.

Today was Day 162 of running in a row. I've now run, on consecutive days, a complete Major League Baseball season.

Sunday, June 12, 2022
   Day 163 – 2.0 miles

The rock band Styx once had a song titled *Nothing Ever Goes As Planned*. If ever there was a title for today, that would have been it.

The day was supposed to begin with me pitching with my whole family in attendance. Ethan was also going to be my catcher. It would have been great. Ethan and I got to the field early, but the game was postponed due to rain as was the "Walk-Off for Dr. Sem" celebration. Late yesterday, they called that off due to the forecast.

Ryan and Tiffany left early because Ryan was having terrible abdominal pain. They drove immediately to their local hospital. Ryan had appendicitis and his appendix was immediately removed. He's doing fine. Thank God.

My back hurts as does my right calf. The calf pain is definitely due to all the dancing on Friday. I am concerned because I have to do all the dancing again tomorrow for our second Field Day.

As I reflected on the day, I wanted to feel sorry for myself. A lot did not go right today. But then I thought about all the good and considered some other words

from *The Lord's Prayer*, "*Give us this day our daily bread...*". I have been given my daily bread, and so much more, and in abundance.

Maybe the best aspect of my running prayers is that they keep me thinking about the words I say, not only when I am saying them, but throughout the day as well.

Monday, June 13, 2022
Day 164 – 1.1 miles

I woke up with my back still hurting. I iced it, but I didn't get much relief. Worse than that, my right calf is in pain. This is just about in the spot where I had the surgery on my Achilles tendon in 2020. I know this came from all the dancing, and I'm concerned because I have to dance all morning again today.

To get my run in, I stayed on the softer TM and took the easy way out. I almost feel guilty counting one mile as a run. The higher miles will come again. Today, I'm just looking to survive.

I knew the day would come when I pushed my body too far. I'm now there. The next question will be how quickly I can heal.

Tuesday, June 14, 2022
    Day 165 – 2.1 miles

Yesterday, I did all the dances and then my right calf hurt all day. I reached out to my physical therapist, but she has no openings this week. I'll have to be smart and not overdo it. I am stretching a lot, icing, and using the Hypervolt to hopefully help the area heal.

Because one mile feels so much like cheating, I did two slow miles today. To be honest, two miles also feels a bit like cheating.

When I'm not as active as I'd like to be, for example, when I'm injured, I feel differently as a person. I don't feel complete. After the surgery, when I couldn't run, I would feel this overall sadness when I'd pass certain places where I enjoyed running. Worse, when I'd see other runners outside, I'd be jealous of them. I wondered how they could be doing something I could only dream of. In a sense, this sport is an obsession. When I can't do as I wish physically, it brings me down. I cannot imagine what old age will be like.

Injuries hurt more in ways more than just physically.

Wednesday, June 15, 2022
    Day 166 – 2.0 miles

I am still taking it easy.

We had a baseball game last night, but I didn't get in. It was probably for the best. Sitting on the bench for an entire game reminded me of when I "played" high school ball. My ball playing days consisted mostly of watching from the sidelines. Since I didn't play in many games, I learned how to juggle baseballs to pass the time.

Thursday, June 16, 2022
  Day 167 – 3.1 miles

My calf is slowly feeling better. Discretion being the better part of valor, I'm glad I've been smart this week with my runs. I am sure my entire body is appreciating this little respite.

Today I was able to push the distance a little. I wasn't fast, but it's progress.

Tonight, Ethan and I are going to see Paul McCartney in concert.

Friday, June 17, 2022
  Day 168 – 4.1 miles

The concert last night was amazing. Bruce Springsteen made a surprise appearance. Ethan and I have now been to Met Life Stadium two times this year. We have seen the greatest football player (Tom Brady) and the greatest living musical artist (Paul McCartney). Not bad!

My body seems to be healing itself rather well. I pushed the distance a little more today and don't seem to be any worse for the wear.

Saturday, June 18, 2022
  Day 169 – 4.4 miles

Laurie and Ethan were out most of the day so after my early morning walk and podcast, I found myself alone and in a literal fog for most of the day. The reality of the fact that my career is just about over has hit me hard. Last night was our retirement dinner which was a wonderful. The staff presented me with gifts and a book of letters that reduced me to tears when I read them last night (and again this morning). The speeches were heart-felt. I am going to miss these people terribly. For fourteen years, I opened up my life to them, and they opened their lives to me. Now I'll no longer be part of their daily lives. It's harrowing to know all of this.

My whole being was encumbered with sadness, melancholy, emptiness, and loneliness. I had no energy. I felt completely empty. I was a shell of a human being and wondered, and worried if this is what retirement will feel like.

I checked my e-mails (as I always do) all day. No one wrote. Why would they? I'm yesterday's story.

My replacement as principal was named yesterday. I'm thrilled with the choice—a colleague who has been a vice principal at the middle school for a long time. I know she will do a great job. The plan will be for us to work together all summer to make a smooth transition. It is strange knowing that my school is no longer really mine.

I hoped that my daily run would do me good. And it did. I didn't run fast, but when I left home, I thought I'd maybe cover two miles, and instead, I reached 4.4 miles. I ran on roads that I had never been on before which made the journey especially nice.

Running can lift me when I need it most. For the forty minutes I was outside I started to feel some contentment in knowing that I did my job well. Yet, once the run finished, and the endorphins went away, and alone at home, I spent much of the day crying.

Sunday, June 19, 2022
Day 170 – 2.0 miles

I got my run in, just two miles on the TM, early – before our baseball game in Jersey City. I pitched six innings, did well, and earned the win.

One of my favorite annual activities is having a catch with my dad on Father's Day. My dad is 83 years-old, but he can still play ball. It's amazing. One of the things I plan to do a lot of in retirement is have catches with my dad. There are certain things in life that are priceless. That is one of them.

Monday, June 20, 2022
Day 171 – 2.0 miles

As it all winds down, I am full of conflicting emotions. I often seem to have no energy for my daily runs.

Tuesday, June 21, 2022
Day 172 – 4.1 miles

I found the energy to reach four miles. I don't know how.

Wednesday, June 22, 2022
Day 173 – 3.1 miles

Yesterday we had our fifth-grade graduation ceremony. On two different occasions, the parents all stood and applauded for me. At one point, I didn't think I would be able to get through it all and asked a teacher to be on stand-by in case I couldn't read the names of the students as they passed across the stage one last time, but I held it together, if barely.

Today is my last day as a principal with students. This is difficult. I knew it would be hard—almost impossible. Everything seems heavy.

I reached three miles on the TM and stopped. I don't want to have a heart attack on the day I go out as principal.

Thursday, June 23, 2022
    Day 174 – 4.1 miles

With a heavy heart and empty insides and a being completely numb, I gathered myself to run on the TM before heading to Hawes for my last day with my staff.

***

Yesterday there was a surprise parade through the halls of the school for the two retiring teachers and me. At the end of the parade, the Home and School Association Presidents presented me a large box full of letters and cards from parents and students, past and present.

Once I returned home, I started reading the cards and letters. These told the tale of my career. They were filled with words of sincere love and thanks.

One letter began:
    I am sitting in my dorm room at college and my roommate is wondering why I am crying as I write a letter to my elementary school principal...

It took me hours to read each of the letters. Some were pages long.

My number one goal as a principal was to establish a school as a place where students could be happy and enjoy learning. I wanted to create a school based on kindness and respect and love. I guess I succeeded. I also know though that the heroes in my school are the teachers. It's always been that way. I was simply the beneficiary of being surrounded by greatness.

My body is an empty shell right now exhausted from the emotions of the last few days. We have a baseball game tonight. I hope it's rained out.

Friday, June 24, 2022
    Day 175 – 4.0 miles

I keep thinking about all the things that mattered a lot, but no longer matter at all. Hundreds of things. Thousands. For more than a quarter-century, I had the weight of so much on my shoulders. But now it's over. The things that were my problem, aren't.

***

I pitched last night and had one of the worst games of my life. We lost. It was ugly. I had nothing. I tried. But I was an empty shell and because of that, I got shelled.

***

Laurie and I will get away to the beach for the weekend alone. It'll be quiet there, but it's a different quiet. That's a quiet I am used to. It's a quiet I need right now.

***

I ran four miles today, outside. I have to go to work, I'll be working all summer, but I have nothing to rush into the office for any longer. I didn't want to run today.

I don't care about this stupid streak right now.

Saturday, June 25, 2022
Day 176 – 3.0 miles

Last night I woke up with a terrible cough that left my throat raw. I was up for about an hour in the middle of the night and never quite felt myself through much of the morning.

Laurie wanted to go to the beach library so I rode down in the car with her, but instead of riding back, I ran home. Anything to get the run in.

Sunday, June 26, 2022
Day 177 – 3.0 miles

I still don't feel 100%. It's not easy to run when you can't breathe, but I continue to push myself forward. I stayed close to the beach house which made the effort tedious.

I am way behind where I thought I'd be at this point in my running. These last few weeks have beaten me up.

Monday, June 27, 2022
Day 178 – 4.2 miles

Back home again and running on the roads that are most familiar to me, I remembered a run from years ago that made me understand what it must be like to be a professional boxer. On that run, my mind must have been elsewhere, because I ran, head-first, into a wide low-hanging tree branch. The next thing I knew, I was on the sidewalk, slowly waking up. The branch must have knocked me out for at least a moment. As I slowly came to my senses and realized what happened, I likened my experience to what a fighter must feel when he's knocked to the canvas. I didn't even see it coming...

Tuesday, June 28, 2022
Day 179 – 3.1 miles

Still not back to full health, I figured that I'd put my old theory to the test. I decided to sweat this lingering cold out of my body. First, I soaked in the hot tub to get my body temperature up. I then put on a bunch of layers and ran three somewhat hard miles on the TM. After the run, I soaked again in the hot tub.

As the day progressed my runny nose stopped and the cough all but went away.

Maybe I'm on to something.

Wednesday, June 29, 2022
Day 180 – 5.0 miles

I planned to run twice today to reach 100 miles for the month. I have today off so my first run came in the mid-morning. Everything felt good and strong and light. The miles went by with relative ease.

I then got busy with other tasks, like writing, and the day escaped me. Ethan bought Mexican food home for dinner. And after that, there was no way I was running.

Thursday, June 30, 2022
   Day 181 – 3.0 miles

Today is the last day of June which seems like it should be the half-way point in the year, but it's not. I still have 184 days to go before 2022 is history.

Today is Laurie and my 31st wedding anniversary. She is the best thing that ever happened to me.

We're all meeting at the beach: my in-laws (Laurie is driving them), all the boys, and Tiffany and Perri. It'll be a full house and it will be great. I hate traffic so I left at 6:40 a.m. to get to the beach quicker.

Alone at the beach, I covered the miles to reach 100 for the month. I was running somewhat quickly (about 9-minute-mile pace) for the first two miles and then decided to really push the final mile completing it in 7:42.

I'm starting to feel like my old self again.

JULY

"It's about a willingness to cross boundaries."
Peter Tegen

Friday, July 1, 2022
    Day 182 – 7.0 miles

It is now getting close to the point where I must begin my 16-week training program to prepare for the New York City Marathon in November. I set out at 8:00 a.m. with the goal of equaling my longest run of 2022—seven miles.

In a typical year, I would have had a few 10-mile runs under my belt by now. Since I don't, I'm going to have to ratchet it up a little quicker than usual.

The daily running has impacted my ability to run longer distances. I haven't pushed my body hard enough on most days knowing I'd have to run again the next day. I also haven't worked on speed drills like I used to. I'm always thinking about the next day's run, which, in some regards, isn't the best thing as I begin my training.

I felt great for much of the run, but the final two miles were long and slow. When I arrived back at the beach house, the sweat was literally pouring off me.

When I come home from a run, I'd like for my wife to say, "You look so strong and powerful." Instead, I got something else. Laurie told me that I was gross.

Saturday, July 2, 2022
 Day 183 – 3.0 miles

I'm now past the halfway point in my year-long running quest. I don't know if I completed the more difficult part or, with a marathon looming, if the worst is yet to come. In some sense, I think the worst is behind me. I have proven to myself that I can run every day for months on end. Now all I need to do is maintain the pace. The biggest challenge will be that my mileage will have to increase by leaps and bounds so I can be ready for the big race in November.

This morning I ran well before anyone else woke up. As I covered the miles, I thought a lot about the things that had given me great stress at work. There's one road down here at the beach that has the same name of a person I had to fire a long time ago. I remembered the angst that caused me at the time. I am finding it to be a challenge to understand that I am not responsible for the decisions at my school any longer, they have been so much a part of my daily thoughts, that I can't seem to let them go.

Sunday, July 3, 2022
 Day 184 – 4.0 miles

Ryan is unable to run following his appendectomy, but Tiffany wanted to get a few miles in, so she and I ran together.

Monday, July 4, 2022
 Day 185 – 5.0 miles

I didn't feel much like running today. I knew I didn't have a choice, I had to run, but I was not looking forward to getting outside nor covering the miles. Sometimes running every day is a real drag, but even when I hate the runs, I'm getting through them.

I developed a mantra when training for one of my first marathons which helped me greatly often when I was at my lowest points. I said, simply, "Every step means a great deal." I'd repeat it over and over until I got to a point, and usually not long after, where I fell into a good rhythm that carried me over until the next time I struggled, usually a few miles down the road. That short saying distracted me from the pain I was in and provided some necessary focus. I knew that with a bit more effort, that I'd be accomplishing something worthy by completing the run rather than quitting.

Tuesday, July 5, 2022
Day 186 – 6.0 miles

The one thing that I don't like about the beach house is the bed we sleep on. It's much too soft for me. It's always only a matter of time before the soft mattress causes my lower back to hurt.

I didn't want to run again, but I did, of course, and once I got out there and loosened up a bit, I felt good.

I'm not sure if the reason I haven't wanted to run lately is that I'm still mentally exhausted from the whirlwind of the last few months or if I am just developing a hatred of running.

Wednesday, July 6, 2022
Day 187 – 3.0 miles

Home again and this was the closest I have come to giving up this whole running everyday thing.

After leaving the beach early, working all day with the new principal, and spending some time visiting with my parents, I didn't get outside to run until 7:45 p.m. I went out reluctantly and was grumpy the whole time.

My back hurt all day and after the run I soaked in the hot tub, but it didn't bring much relief.

I'll see the chiropractor tomorrow. It can't come soon enough.

Thursday, July 7, 2022
Day 188 – 4.1 miles

Back hurting, I still banged out four miles on the TM. This gives me a little confidence. If I do four miles each day the rest of the week, I'll be back to a 30-mile week.

Friday, July 8, 2022
Day 189 – 3.1 miles

I went to the chiropractor and to physical therapy, but neither provided immediate relief. I had a baseball game last night, but I didn't pitch. I was in the "bullpen" and they never needed me. I have this fear that people will think I'm not strong if I don't play, so if they asked, I would have pitched through the pain. I'm glad they didn't need me.

I'm sure the daily running is aggravating my back. The smart thing to do would be to just quit. I gave it my best efforts. It might just be that my body wasn't meant to do this.

On the other hand, I know when I feel better in a day or two, or in a week, I'll be so mad at myself for failing that I cannot allow quitting to be an option.

This morning I soaked in the hot tub before my run and again selected the treadmill since it is softer than the roads. After running, I iced my back for 20 minutes before heading for a quiet day alone in my school office. Each day I bring a few items home and then put them away so I don't end up with tons of boxes of stuff at the end of the summer.

Saturday, July 9, 2022
Day 190 – 3.1 miles

We're heading back out to Hershey, and with the looming car ride, which always aggravates my back, I was reluctant to run more than a mile, but, pride, or ego, or something got the better of me and I ran three miles on the TM. I started the run out at only 5.0 MPH, but slowly increased the speed. Still, I fell just short of 30 miles for the week by ending at 28.3 miles.

Sunday, July 10, 2022
Day 191 – 4.0 miles

Yesterday was a great day. Ryan gave me an adjustment at his chiropractic office and the pain went away for a good long while.

I woke up today, still stiff and slightly less sore. The bed we slept on was soft which is never good for me when I have a bad back. I spent the last few hours of the night sleeping on the floor. I do that at home sometimes too.

Later in the morning, Ryan, Tiffany, and I went for a run on one of the beautiful paved trails near their home. It's great when communities set aside tons of land for recreation. At the 1.5 mile mark (or so), Ryan wanted to take me on one of the killer hills he works out on. Tiffany went back a somewhat easier way.

It was great while it lasted.

After the run, my lower back killed all day. We went to the Hershey Gardens and I sat through most of it as Laurie, Ryan, Tiffany, and Ethan strolled the beautiful grounds. We then drove home.

Last night, I slept on the floor on a folding travel mattress. I hoped that the firmer surface would help.

Monday, July 11, 2022
Day 192 – 2.0 miles

Still, in pain, I decided that I would use the only loophole I can think of in order to get through this misery and continue my daily running. I cannot quit. I cannot see any way in which I would ever forgive myself for quitting. Throughout my life, I have always felt I was stronger than pain—and I have been. I cannot let this current hurdle thwart what I have worked so hard to attain.

In order to accomplish running each day, but also to find the most time for rest, I took most of the day off and did two slow miles at 11:40 p.m.

Tuesday, July 12, 2022
Day 193 – 2.0 miles

To celebrate the start of my 54th birthday, I ran two miles starting at 12:05 a.m. I then went to bed knowing I'll have close to 36 hours of rest ahead of me.

Wednesday, July 13, 2022
Day 194 – 3.0 miles

My initial hope was to run late again tonight, but I had to get my run in before work because I am having a colonoscopy tomorrow. Because of the preparation for that procedure, I'm not permitted to have any solid food today.

My back still hurts more than it should. I don't understand why this pain has lingered for so long.

Thursday, July 14, 2022
Day 195 – 3.1 miles

A colonoscopy is a routine procedure, but in the preparation area, they hooked me up to a heart monitor, a blood pressure monitor, and gave me an IV. I don't get concerned when I'm having a medical procedure performed, including the surgery I had on my Achilles. I always have full faith in my doctors. Still, with all of these precautions, it seemed like they were taking me to open heart surgery.

I remember when my orthopedist called after he reviewed an MRI to let me know that he'd have to operate on my Achilles. He said, "The tears are pretty bad and getting worse." I replied, "Good!" That shocked the doctor. "Good?" he questioned. "No, it's bad. I'll have to operate." I said, "Yes, that's what I want. I want you to fix me so I can run well again."

After the procedure today, I took a nap and was out of sorts for much of the day. I didn't run until 7:00 p.m. I ran slowly on the TM because Laurie didn't want me outside in the heat. You're not supposed to operate heavy machinery within 24 hours of having anesthesia, but they say nothing about running on it...

***

My back feels better and I'm off from work tomorrow, so I hope to get a longer run in. I need to get back to who I am and need to be as a runner.

Friday, July 15, 2022
Day 196 – 5.1 miles

Right before bed, I experienced a different type of back pain. More sharp pains, but this time in my lower right back, not in the center where the pain has been. I didn't sleep much again.

I am beginning to wonder if the running is worth it.

I went to my chiropractor and talked to him about my efforts to run every day. He understands athletes, but more, he understands me. I have been going to him since the early 1990s. He looked at me and said, "Keep running."

A few hours later, I ran 5.1 miles to reach 24,901 lifetime miles. I have been chasing this goal for years. Why is this a significant number? It's the circumference, in miles, of the Earth at the equator. I have now run enough miles in my lifetime to make it all the way around the world!

Saturday, July 16, 2022
Day 197 – 3.28 miles

The sixteen-week marathon training begins tomorrow. It's now "big league" time. I start to think of the effort this is going to take, the countless hours running, and the pain that accompanies it all.

I'm starting to think of all sorts of quotes such as, "You are tomorrow what you work for today," and (one of my favorites), "Pain is temporary, pride is forever."

Sunday, July 17, 2022
Day 198 – 3.1 miles

And so it begins…

It seems strange that the first Sunday of November is 16-weeks away. My 23rd marathon and my 9th NYC marathon beckon in the not-too-far distance.

I pitched today and did really well. I went six innings. I gave up four runs. We won the game. My back (finally) felt good, and my arm did as well.

Following the game was the "Dr. Sem Walk-Off Celebration" at Yogi Berra Stadium which had been postponed from June. Over 400 people from my school community attended. They all wore baseball jerseys with "DR. SEM" and my uniform number 2 on the back.

I threw out the ceremonial first pitch. It was a strike. The love from this community that has been showered on me has been tremendous. I was glad that Laurie, Alex, Perri, Ethan, and my parents were able to be there and see it all.

After a long and wonderful day, at 9:00 p.m., elated, I did three miles on the treadmill.

Monday, July 18, 2022
   Day 199 – 4.1 miles

This morning I felt good. The back pain seems gone and my arm also doesn't hurt. I ran on the TM before work.

There have been a lot of days these last few weeks where I did not want to run, but, in reflection, the runs might be what has kept me balanced. Running provides a sense of normalcy to my life. I know each day, at some point, I need to put my running clothes on, stretch, limber-up, and then get on the treadmill or get outside and get moving.

As so much in my life has changed, the one thing that hasn't is running.

Tuesday, July 19, 2022
   Day 200 – 3.1 miles

There have been days when I don't think I'll be able to finish my yearlong running journey, but I am very confident I can do it now. I have pushed through days when the pain in my back has been excruciating. I have overcome apathy. I have forced myself to run even when I couldn't imagine getting on the treadmill or going outside. It's only July, but by reaching my 200th consecutive day of running, I feel like I am on the back stretch. I know that I will reach my goal by simply going day by day. When big tasks are broken into smaller bits, they become more attainable. A person can't run 365 days in one day, but he can do it by going one day at a time all year long.

I'm well on my way.

Wednesday, July 20, 2022
Day 201 – 4.1 miles

Laurie and Ethan surprised me by hanging a "gallery shelf" in my home office. Laurie invented this idea as a way for me to be able to display and rotate some of the many framed pictures and items I have - especially with so many items coming home from my office at school.

I ran fast on the TM today and am noticing a trend. I get faster and faster, seemingly stronger and stronger, and then I find myself hurt again. I have to be smart going forward because with the marathon on the (distant) horizon, I can't afford to have weeks like last week where I was hobbled and compromised by pain.

Thursday, July 21, 2022
Day 202 – 4.35 miles

I was finally back outside for my run. I greatly enjoyed running in the early morning heat. I'll head into the office, as I have been doing all summer long, but I have no urgency.

The new principal and I have been working closely for a few weeks now. She is the perfect person to take over running the school. She is kind and patient. She understands teachers and students. She smiles a lot. And she's a deep thinker—much deeper than me. The school will be in great hands.

My dad turns 84 today. I hope I am as strong as he is when I reach his age.

Friday, July 22, 2022
    Day 203 – 3.0 miles

I wanted to get my run in quickly today before Laurie and I headed out to Baltimore for a book talk I am giving at the Babe Ruth Museum.

I did three miles outside. Each mile was a little faster than the one before it which, I believe, helps me in my marathon training. I always fade in the upper miles of a marathon. One way to try to beat that trend is to run negative splits (quicker and quicker miles) each time I head out. The idea is to be able to run stronger when I'm most tired. This may seem counter-intuitive, but it makes sense to me. If I can run hard when I feel like quitting, I will do better when the going gets difficult in the marathon.

Saturday, July 23, 2022
    Day 204 – 3.0 miles

We spent the night in Hunt Valley, Maryland at an Embassy Suites Hotel in a place similar to every other area where hotels are found outside all major cities. There are malls and condos and business properties all over. This is America today. All of these "communities" look the same. They have the same stores, the same restaurants, and the same hotel chains. Areas like this aren't great for running. It seems that everywhere you go there is a sign stating very clearly "PRIVATE PROPERTY." Everyone and everything is unwelcoming.

I ran on the quiet corporate boulevard (titled International Way, which is what all these roads are named) outside the hotel. I encountered one sterile environment after the next—a corporate park, a hotel, and a retirement community, one after the next, almost in repetition. It all made for a very boring and very unsatisfactory early morning run.

Sunday, July 24, 2022
  Day 205 – 6.1 miles

It was great to be a speaker at the
Babe Ruth Museum yesterday.
There are times when I feel like
someone important when I go to
places to talk about my books. I
doubt I'll ever be a television or
movie star, or a famous athlete,
but I am a published author, and
it is fun when people see my
books and ask, with some awe,
"You wrote that book?"

The museum set me up in a room
that gets regular visitor traffic so
as I spoke, visitors came in and
out of the room. That made me
feel less famous and more irrel-
evant, but it was a great experience, nonetheless.

Back home this morning, Laurie and I drove home yesterday after
the author talk, I began the day as a relief pitcher coming into the
game, a slugfest, in the third inning. We were down 9-8. I surren-
dered only one run over six innings. Ethan hit a booming triple. Our
bats stayed hot while I cooled the other team off. We won 20-10.

I got my run in as I watched the Yankees on TV. It's extremely hot
right now and Laurie prefers that in the heat, I run inside on the
treadmill. I don't push back at these small requests. Laurie is very
understanding of this year-long obsession of mine. I also have to admit that I'm not young any longer. I don't think of myself as old, but
guys my age do suffer from heart attacks. My dad did when he was
52. I do have to face reality. I'm not sure how many years of running
I have left in me. This makes completing this year by running every
day that much more urgent in my mind.

Monday, July 25, 2022
  Day 206 – 6.1 miles

Sometimes a runner just feels it. Everything seems to work. Today I felt strong and able. I did my fastest six-miler yet. My mind was focused, and I felt great. Now that the back pain from a few weeks ago is completely gone, I feel like a new person. This is how I perform when I'm full of confidence for the marathon.

I feel strong and able and focused. I feel like I could run forever. I wish I could capture this kind of confidence every time I run.

Tuesday, July 26, 2022
  Day 207 – 3.1 miles

I need to remind myself to not overdo it right now. Today, after my Tuesday walk, I did a fast three miles on the TM. I plan to get outside to run tomorrow, but I was a little rushed as I wanted to get to work quickly to continue working with the new principal. I am enjoying all of our discussions about education, philosophy, teaching, children, and so much more. She is going to be an outstanding principal. I am so thrilled that I'm being replaced by someone great.

Wednesday, July 27, 2022
  Day 208 – 4.1 miles

It is difficult for me to remember how badly I felt just a week or so ago, because I feel great. I went out this morning for an easy run, and instead felt strong and able and ran negative splits throughout. My last mile was under eight-minute-mile pace. I never intended to run that fast today. I've done this a few times this year and I am amazed that I can still cover miles that quickly.

Thursday, July 28, 2022
  Day 209 – 3.1 miles

I didn't overdo it today. I covered the miles slowly to give my body a much needed break.

Friday, July 29, 2022
Day 210 – 4.5 miles

I again didn't overdo it again because tomorrow, I plan to run eight miles, my longest distance of the year. I have to ramp up the mileage now. These training weeks are the keys to marathon success. One wins the race (all finishers are winners) by putting the effort into the training.

There were a lot of people walking dogs this morning. I always cross the street or get as far away from the dogs as I can. Some people have very little control of their pets and I never like dogs, especially large ones, jumping towards me, especially if they are barking, even if they are leashed.

Saturday, July 30, 2022
Day 211 – 8.15 miles

According to my marathon plan, I don't have to reach eight miles until two weeks from today, but I like to always be ahead of schedule when it comes to the long runs.

Today I covered the distance on the "hills of home." I did well through six, keeping a steady pace. Miles seven and eight were tough, but I made it through them. Long runs like this give me confidence and so much of running is simply me believing in myself. A positive mindset leads to positive results.

My back has felt great. Thank God. A few weeks ago, Ryan recommended that I do McKenzie stretches. The exercises Ryan gave me are made up of a series of simple floor movements designed to stretch out my lower back. I have been doing these almost every day for a few weeks now and they are working.

The eight-miles helped me reach 35-miles this week—my best week this year!

Sunday, July 31, 2022
   Day 212 – 3.1 miles

I have now finished seven months. I have completed 58.3% of this journey.

Earlier today, before my baseball game, I rode the bike for 30-minutes. Then I was the starting pitcher and gave up five runs in five innings. I wasn't very good. I took the loss. Sometimes a pitcher simply doesn't have it. Today, I did not.

I got my run in late (at 8:30 p.m.) and ran three somewhat hard miles. It was a good way to end the month.

AUGUST

"When I finish a run, every part of me is smiling."
Jeff Galloway

Monday, August 1, 2022
   Day 213 – 5.0 miles

I woke up early and set to work to finish the first draft of the Roy White book. Seven to eight hours later, I was done and going a bit stir crazy because I hadn't yet run or exercised in any way.

One thing I don't think most people understand is that writing is a job. No, most authors don't make tons of money, but to do it well takes a tremendous amount of time and effort. We write, read, revise, rewrite, reread, revise, and start again. And again. The distractions are many. The doorbell rings. The phone rings. Someone has something to say. We lose our train of thought.

With the first draft of the Roy White book completed, I did my stretches, loosened up, and set out on my run. I planned to do three miles, but I felt great, possibly from finishing my latest manuscript, and was able to push myself and reach five miles.

Tuesday, August 2, 2022
   Day 214 – 4.1 miles

On August 2, 1979, Thurman Munson, the catcher on the New York Yankees, died in a terrible plane crash. I was eleven-years-old when it happened and didn't understand how a Major League baseball player could be dead. These ballplayers were superheroes to me, no different than Batman or Superman. Superheroes didn't die. How could a New York Yankee who I had just seen playing die? It all made no sense. As I look back on that day, I realize that a significant part of the innocence of my childhood was lost that day.

A little over a month later, my grandfather, who was never sick, and was out square dancing, died suddenly. In a profound way, my life was forever changed. I realized that life isn't forever.

After my early-morning Tuesday walk, and a few hours of writing due to revisions I needed to make in Roy's book, I went out for a mid-day run. I usually prefer to run earlier in the day, but to get outside and run after hours of writing is something uniquely special and rewarding.

Wednesday, August 3, 2022
  Day 215 – 3.1 miles

Our starting catcher brought Jolly Rancher candies to our game last night. I put a candy in my mouth as he came to bat. He homered. When he came up the next time, I ate another Jolly Rancher. He promptly hit a 3-run homer. The next inning he came up with the bases loaded. I ate another candy. He hit a grand slam. Amazing! We won in going away fashion. I forget the exact score, but it was something like a million to nothing. (I might be exaggerating a little.)

Thursday, August 4, 2022
  Day 216 – 5.1 miles

I set out today for an easy run. After one mile, I saw that my pace was 9:05. That was faster than I felt I was running, but when that happens, my competitive spirit kicks in. I think, "If I ran that fast while running slowly, I can crush this." And I did. When I can run like this, with power, energy, speed, and confidence, I feel superhuman.

The key for me going forward is finding the way to harness this positive mindset more often.

Friday, August 5, 2022
Day 217 – 3.0 miles

Running is a challenge that confronts me every day. I am forced to ask myself if I will be strong or weak on a daily basis.

Today I was weak. I did not want to run. My mind wasn't into it; my legs either. I did get out there, but my overall performance was terrible. I ran miserably. What frustrates me even more than the poor run is the fact that yesterday's run was so great. It has been a big struggle for me to find any sense of consistency.

Saturday, August 6, 2022
Day 218 – 5.0 miles + 5.1 miles

Saturdays have always been the days for my long training runs for the marathon. I like to get out early and get the run in. The problem is I have two podcasts on Saturdays that take up most of my morning.

According to my marathon plan, today's long run called for seven miles, a distance I exceeded last week when I ran eight. I wanted to do ten miles, but I didn't have the time to invest in a long run like that today. I determined today to cover ten miles in a different way...

There is a theory that two shorter runs can benefit the body in the same way as one longer run. I'm not sure if I believe that, but since we had to do some work at my in-laws in Ho-Ho-Kus, New Jersey (five miles away), I figured I would put this theory to the test. I would run to my in-laws, and later, I'd run back home.

The run to Ho-Ho-Kus was very tough because today was oppressively hot. When I arrived, I knew that there was no way I could run home in that heat. Instead, I drove home with Ethan feeling a bit like I had failed.

This gnawed at me for the remainder of the day, so I got on the TM at 8:00 p.m. to get the second five-mile run in.

Sunday, August 7, 2022
    Day 219 – 3.1 miles

Today was a whirlwind of a day. In our final baseball game of the season, I pitched the final five innings, but the game was already lost at that point. We got clobbered.

More than the game, though, I feel like a very meaningful part of my life has come to an end. If all goes according to his hopes and wishes, this game was possibly the last time Ethan and I would ever play baseball on a team together. It's been four remarkable years. It's been a dream for me to play baseball at a competitive level with my son. If all goes well for him, Ethan should have a job by next year and he may not be living in the area.

I've said goodbye to a lot this year. This was just the latest thing. I loved playing baseball with Ethan as my teammate. I did something with him that most fathers and sons never have the chance to do. It's been a magical ride.

I then spent a few hours with Roy White getting some last bits of information for our book. Following our discussion, I went back to the manuscript to add in the new material and then read the entire thing one more time. Writing is a long and sometimes (often times) arduous process. I love writing, but it isn't always fun.

In all of this, I almost forgot about running. I didn't get on the TM until 9:00 p.m. This was the closest I came to missing a run this year.

Monday, August 8, 2022
    Day 220 – 3.1 miles

I had to do the TM again as I had an early dental appointment to get a cavity filled before heading off to work.

My dentist always brings a positive approach to every encounter. He is, genuinely, one of the most positive and upbeat people I have ever known. Positive people bring out the best in me. It's great to be around joyful people.

When my dentist has to fill a cavity for me though, he doesn't always smile because I don't take any Novocain. As a result, he is always afraid that he's going to hurt me. When the process is over, the dentist always smiles and breathes deeply. Me too.

Tuesday, August 9, 2022
    Day 221 – 3.1 miles

It's been a furnace outside, so I decided to use the TM today.

I decided to really push myself today, to try to be very fast. I was hoping to break twenty-four minutes, under eight-minute-mile pace for three miles, but fell just short finishing at 24:03.

When I am pushing myself hard like this, I don't think of myself as a 54-year-old man. I feel young and energetic and strong and powerful. I believe this helps keep me as young as I can be.

Wednesday, August 10, 2022
    Day 222 – 4.25 miles

My days at work are packed with long and wonderful discussions. The new principal and I are discussing everything—all the various things that make our school the most wonderful one there is anywhere. I was never before part of a transition like this, but it's been wonderful to have all of this time, basically the entire summer, together.

After work, I exercised caution and ran at a comfortable, but not fast, pace outside. I am trying to keep everything in balance, so I don't sustain an injury that ends this quest and jeopardizes the marathon. I've come much too far to fail.

Thursday, August 11, 2022
Day 223 – 12 miles

Laurie and I are back at the beach for a few days with my in-laws, and I awoke today to a thunderstorm that I hoped wouldn't get in the way of the long run I hoped to accomplish.

The skies cleared up by 8:00 a.m. and I set out to do a ten-miler on a route that brings me to and from the boardwalk at Seaside Heights. This is one of my favorite long beach runs. Being on the boardwalk gives me the sense that I am far from home and someplace very special. I always feel like a child again filled with the wonder of cotton candy, candy apples, and the possibility of winning prizes on games of chance.

At ten miles, I still felt great and kept going, adding a few more miles to my overall effort. This was a huge confidence builder.

I am reminded again that I can do more than I think is possible.

Friday, August 12, 2022
Day 224 – 5.1 miles

One of my biggest concerns as I move forward with my marathon training is how my body will respond the day after a long run. I wondered especially how I'd respond today. Getting to twelve miles yesterday was a big jump in my mileage.

I went out very slowly to see what I could do. First one step, then the next. I found that I moved easily. My legs weren't sore. My back wasn't tight. Everything seemed in order.

I covered five miles to reach thirty miles for the week.

I was elated, feeling like everything had finally come together when, within moments of returning to the beach house, my father-in-law lost consciousness.

Laurie was right there with him and caught him as he fell over from his chair and helped him to the ground. Laurie kept talking to him as he slowly regained consciousness. I called 911 as Laurie served as a pillar of strength for her mom, the paramedics, and her dad as he was rushed to the hospital.

Saturday, August 13, 2022
Day 225 – 3.25 miles

My mother-in-law and Laurie will spend most of the day at the hospital. My brother-in-law, Mark, is mentally challenged. I will be with him at the house making sure he is fine. This is usually my role in situations like this.

While I had the chance, before Laurie left for the hospital, I got my run in. In order to complete this running challenge, I sometimes have to be selfish.

Sunday, August 14, 2022
Day 226 – 6.1 miles

I got up early with the thought about pushing for another ten-miler today, but as I headed out, my legs were tired and very heavy. I didn't want to get too far from home and conk out, especially since I needed to be around to help everyone else. Staying near home, I took it mile-by-mile to see if I could run some life back into my legs and ended up reaching six miles.

As I ran, I decided that my goal for the week would be to run six miles each day. If I can reach that goal, it would get me to my first 40-mile week, which is essential in my marathon training.

***

My father-in-law was released from the hospital. He's back with us at the beach house. Thank God.

I won't be staying at the beach past tomorrow morning. If only for a few more weeks, I have a job to report to on Monday morning.

Monday, August 15, 2022
Day 227 – 4.1 miles

I was up before 4:00 a.m. and on the road at 4:14 to head home from the beach.

Once home, I ran outside (with the intention to run again later) before heading off to work.

Unfortunately, I had less motivation to run after work and never got that second run accomplished.

Tuesday, August 16, 2022
Day 228 – 3.1 miles + 3.1 miles

I really want to get to forty miles this week, but it is a struggle.

I did three miles on the TM again with the intention to run again later, but I'm probably lying to myself since I never got that second run in yesterday.

Wednesday, August 17, 2022
Day 229 – 5.0 miles

I did manage a second run yesterday, again on the TM. Pushing to a forty-mile week has been tough. I'm not sure if I have it in me yet.

I set out today to cover three miles and ended up doing more. Once I got going, I felt great. I enjoyed the run and wanted it to keep going. It is amazing that I can love and hate the exact same activity from one day to the next and sometimes simultaneously.

Thursday, August 18, 2022
    Day 230 – 4.0 miles

Next Friday is my last day of work. When I'm home and not at my school, it's easy. I'm ready for the next chapter of my life. But, when I'm at my school, as I complete my final tasks in my office and read the e-mails (that still come) from appreciative parents and staff, and as I think of the finality of it all, my eyes fill with tears. I've cried as I have driven home each day. I know I'm leaving a big part of myself behind.

I haven't been sleeping well. When I woke up today, my legs, my arms, and my back were sore. I thought, "I hate running and the aggravation and pain it is causing me."

And I did I hate running, that is until I got outside. Once on the run, I found myself enjoying the sport once again.

Tomorrow we will be back at the beach and I will try to do 15 miles. If I can do that, I'll have a great long run under my belt which will be a huge confidence booster for me. I'll also have my forty-mile week completed.

Friday, August 19, 2022
    Day 231 – 10.1 miles

I didn't reach 15 miles, but I did 10. It was very hot in the early morning sun and I struggled, especially through the final miles.

Even after a shower, I am all uncomfortable. I'm beside myself; miserable, and all out of sorts. I just had a yogurt (good), potato chips (not so good), and a Pepsi (bad) to try to fill my stomach and get some energy. I can't find a place to get comfortable. I'm probably dehydrated.

I was thirsty as I ran, but I wasn't able to get a drink until I was at about mile 8.7 where I bought a Gatorade. At the store, they must have thought I was crazed. I didn't talk. I just sort of staggered in, grabbed a red bottle, and handed money to the girl at the cash register. She gave me my change and I sort of wobbled incoherently out the door. Even with the Gatorade in me, I had to stop and gather myself at about mile nine.

The marathon plan calls for a ten-miler this week. I hit that goal, but to get there, I thoroughly beat myself up.

Saturday, August 20, 2022
Day 232 – 5.0 miles

Coming off a difficult run yesterday, and again on a very hot day, I wanted to make sure to not stray too far from the beach house in case I hit the wall again. I set my mind to five miles and ran up and down all sorts of streets close to home until I reached the requisite distance. With that run, I hit 40-miles for the week. This week was a huge step forward.

Sunday, August 21, 2022
Day 233 – 3.5 miles

I am a firm believer in always striving for bigger and better. I subscribe to the idea of having a growth mindset. If I can do X, I believe I can certainly do X + 1. But, as I have matured, I have also realized that one cannot always push ahead without taking a step backwards sometimes as well.

This week I'm going to back-off a bit. I'm not going to push the miles. Instead, I am going to run shorter distances to give my body a chance to recoup a bit. In regard to the long run, I'll see what Saturday brings when it comes. It might be a tough day following my final exit from school on Friday.

After this week, I'll start to really push the miles. The marathon in November is getting closer and closer.

Monday, August 22, 2022
Day 234 – 3.35 miles

I find myself being a lot more reflective right now. I wonder how quiet it will be in retirement. I also wonder if I will get tired of the new realities that my life will become.

I consider a lot as I run, but running also forces me to live in the moment. I'm often confronted with the desire to quit, or occasionally, push myself farther than I had planned. Being consumed by the immediacy of what I am working through makes running a place where I can escape and just "be."

Tuesday, August 23, 2022
Day 235 – 3.2 miles

The other day at the beach, a few friends came over. We talked about running and I was asked, "What do you do if you don't feel like running one day?" I thought about this for a moment and replied, "I put on my shoes and run."

In the end, it's that simple. We often have to do things that we don't want to do.

What do you do when you don't want to go to work one day? You go to work. You have to. It's your job. This year, I have made running a job. I have to do it every day. I don't give myself a choice.

Wednesday, August 24, 2022
Day 236 – 5.2 miles

I am getting very antsy. I am having a hard time finding any peace.

Today I ran to and around the neighborhood where I grew up and spent a lot of the time remembering old friends, baseball cards, bike rides, my paper routes, and generally feeling sentimental about all that changes over the course of one's life.

Thursday, August 25, 2022
   Day 237 – 4.1 miles

I am actually working hard to take it easy this week. I need to keep reminding myself not to push myself too much. The big weeks with tons of miles are coming. Yet, I am full of nervous energy. I am not sleeping. I need to keep moving.

Friday, August 26, 2022
   Day 238 – 3.3 miles

Today, is my last day as a principal and it feels as if someone handed me Kryptonite.

For fourteen years, I felt a lot like a superhero. As Laurie and I talked about this last night, I said, "When I get in my car and drive away today, whatever superpowers I had will all be gone." I'm turning in my cape and my utility belt.

***

The roads are unsentimental. I found solace, among some tears, as I covered a few miles before heading to my office for the last time.

Saturday, August 27, 2022
   Day 239 – 10.0 miles

Today is the first day of the rest of my life. Yesterday was impossibly difficult. I feel very empty inside and suspect I'll feel this way for a long time.

I always felt it was something special to be the leader of a school and to be trusted with that much authority and responsibility. It was great to give so much love to everyone.

When we give kindness and love, it is returned to us in greater amounts than we ever gave it. I know this all to be true. I've lived this my entire life.

***

The marathon plan called for eleven miles today, and I pushed as best as I could and got close. On one hill, approaching nine miles, I had to walk. That was the first time I walked on a run in a long time.

I reached 32 miles for the week. Going forward, I know I need to be better than this.

Sunday, August 28, 2022
Day 240 – 4.0 miles

I have this fear that in retirement, I'll get lazy. I know that I will have to continually find outlets and avenues to push myself. I am working diligently to make sure that my calendar is full with as many activities as I can plan. Running will be a big part of this transition, but it cannot be my only outlet. Laurie will go back to work soon, and I'll be facing an endless stream of days spent alone.

Monday, August 29, 2022
Day 241 – 8.3 miles

Today is the unofficial first day for many of the teachers. I feel guilty for retiring and not being there to support them. I feel like I should be going to work and that I'm somehow doing the wrong thing.

Feeling out of sorts, I went out for a good long run and defeated a giant hill that I long ago dubbed "The Monster." This hill is the longest and steepest hill in the area. I consider conquering this small mountain an important part of my marathon training. The fact that I climbed that beast of a hill without stopping gives me confidence that I'm on the right track and doing well physically, and more importantly right now, mentally as well.

Tuesday, August 30, 2022
Day 242 – 4.2 miles

I began today by completely forgetting about my Tuesday morning walk. Colin came over to walk with me and I never even knew it. I didn't get to my run until about noon, and about half a mile into the run, I realized that I didn't turn on the Garmin. I felt out of sorts the rest of the way. I hated almost every step of the run and almost quit numerous times.

I hope this is not my new normal.

***

Today is my mother's birthday. She's 83-years-old. Both of my parents are as active as ever. They exercise almost every single day. They serve as a great inspiration to me. If they can do what they're doing in their 80's, I can certainly keep this running challenge going for only a few more months.

Wednesday, August 31, 2022
Day 243 – 7.3 miles

I have a few routes at home that I run that usually signify that I'm getting stronger as a runner. Today's run was through a former IBM office complex in the town of Franklin Lakes. It's a hilly journey, but like The Monster, one I always feel I need to get through as part of my training.

August concludes as my best month of the year. I covered 161.25 miles this month. That's an average of 5.2 miles each day! I also had my first 40-mile week and am on pace to have another this week.

I am two-thirds of the way through this journey. Eight months are completed, I have just four to go.

SEPTEMBER

"It'll be just like starting over."
John Lennon

Thursday, September 1, 2022
Day 244 – 5.0 miles

Today was the first official day for teachers to report to work. A few from my school (my former school) reached out and said they miss me already. It's a sad feeling knowing it's not my school any longer. I still have this sense that I'm doing something wrong by being re-tired. I feel like I should be at work and starting a new year with the staff.

***

My right calf was sore and tight today, so I lifted weights to start the day rather than going for a run.

I'll be teaching a class at Ramapo College this semester, so I attended a meeting there and then ran once I returned home. Ramapo has a large and very hilly campus; I figured the walking there would help loosen up my leg muscles and it did.

Friday, September 2, 2022
Day 245 – 13.1 miles

I made the decision to do my long run today rather than tomorrow. Ryan and Tiffany will be at the beach with us for Labor Day week-end and I do not want to take away time with them to run for hours and hours. Before my run, I went on MapMyRun.com and charted out a somewhat flat route that I could traverse to reach 12 miles and possibly up to 15 miles.

The run went great. I stayed at a solid pace and the miles just peeled off. I was able to remain focused and consistent. I was able to run 13.1 miles, a half-marathon, in a pretty good time of 2:07:13. I didn't push hard, I just stayed within myself and ran.

With the run, I exceeded 40-miles for the week already. I'll hopefully run with Ryan and Tiffany tomorrow. I'd like to do about six miles because there's another milestone ahead...

Saturday, September 3, 2022
Day 246 – 6.5 miles

My favorite runs are the ones we do with the people I love. Ryan and I went out for what was to be a short run, but I knew that if we reached six miles, I would hit 1,000 miles for the year.

We covered the distance, and I passed another milestone.

Of my three sons, my first "running buddy" was Alex. We haven't had many opportunities to run together this year, but back when he was younger and living at home, we ran a few races together. I ran Alex's first half-marathon with him stride for stride for 13.1 miles. Soon after, we partnered together for a relay marathon—each of us running half the distance. On many occasions, Alex rode his bike with me as I ran.

I cherish all these memories.

Sunday, September 4, 2022
Day 247 – 5.0 miles

All yesterday afternoon, I toyed with the idea of going out for a second run. Just two (or so) miles more would have given me a 50-mile week. But, caution, the fear of over-doing it, held me back. I also didn't want to break away from our family time. The fifty-mile weeks will come. We won't see Ryan and Tiffany again until October.

This morning I resolved to run a slow, relaxed, few miles. Five miles later, I was finished. When I got back, I said to Laurie, "Pretty good, right? 247 days in a row." Laurie looked at me with a small smile and simply said, "It fits your personality."

If that means, "focused, determined, and able to achieve goals," I'll take that as a compliment. If it means, "obsessive compulsive and out of my mind," not so much.

Monday, September 5, 2022
Day 248 – 4.1 miles

Today I ran a slow and difficult 4.10 miles. Yesterday we went swimming in the ocean. I don't swim in the ocean very often. As we battled the waves and the tide, I'm sure I used muscles in my legs in ways they haven't been used in a long time. As a result, this morning my legs were very stiff and quite sore. I couldn't get the legs to feel better and as a result my run today uncomfortable and no fun.

Some days I hate this running journey.

Tuesday, September 6, 2022
Day 249 – 3.15 miles

This morning it really hit me. My school is going to open for the students and I'm not going to be there. The finality of it all reality hit home. It is, absolutely, no longer my school.

It rained today which felt very appropriate. The dreariness of the day matched my mood and, as such, I ran outside as the heavens cried with me.

Wednesday, September 7, 2022
   Day 250 – 5.3 miles

I am reaching the point where I can almost begin to realistically consider completing this running journey. The end isn't quite in sight, but it is also not way off in a distance that I cannot comprehend. Two hundred fifty consecutive days of running is an accomplishment I am extremely proud of. I cannot quit. There are no laurels to rest on. This is simply one (albeit big) step in the process.

I loved the run today. I am enjoying the freedom that comes with having lots of free time. The pressure is off. My days are no longer programed by the responsibilities of a job.

Thursday, September 8, 2022
   Day 251 – 9.2 miles

I did an uninspired, but in some ways, remarkable, 9.2 miles this morning. I just kept covering miles and saying to myself, "This isn't really what I want to be doing right now, but I know I have another mile in me."

Running is the most unique of sports. On days when I think I can run forever, I sometimes get nowhere. And on days when I think I have nothing, I can sometimes seemingly run forever.

Friday, September 9, 2022
   Day 252 – 9.4 miles

My baseball team played last night in the playoffs. The game went past midnight. We won. I sat the bench the entire game. Winning is great, but it's not fun if you're not part of it.

Today, I set out again to see how far I could go and once again surpassed nine miles. On my run I discovered a different gigantic hill, one I might have to call "The Monster's Brother."

I also encountered a different monster on the run. As I ran next to a parked pickup truck, a German Sheppard leaped out of the window with a loud bark and a snapped at me. He nearly took my ear off. It scared me half to death.

Saturday, September 10, 2022
Day 253 – 4.25 miles

I gave my body a rest by keeping the mileage lower, yet I reached 40-miles for the second week in a row. I am very pleased!

My first job as a kid was having a newspaper route. I enjoyed having the responsibility of delivering papers two days a week. I also liked having money to spend on baseball cards. I was great at delivering the papers. I was not so great, though, at collecting the newspaper fees from some of the customers. A few customers had very loud and aggressive dogs. Like the German Sheppard yesterday, those dogs frightened me beyond words. I was sure one of them would kill me. As a result, I stopped collecting from some homes. Those families received free newspapers for years because of my refusal to confront their dogs.

Sunday, September 11, 2022
Day 254 – 15.0 miles

I often live in fear of the long run. The aspect of marathon training that I dislike the most isn't the actual running (although it can be very difficult), it's the trepidation that comes from knowing I have to complete a long run. I think about this especially the night before. As I go to sleep, I know that the next day's morning will be filled with pain and there will be times when I am riddled with great doubts about my ability to continue.

I usually don't bring a phone with me on my runs, but I did today, just in case I needed to call Laurie to "rescue" me if I quit the run far from home. In the end, the phone wasn't needed. Over the last seven days, I have now covered more than fifty miles.

This is a significant confidence booster. The marathon is just under two months away and I needed this successful run to keep myself physically as well as mentally on track.

Monday, September 12, 2022
   Day 255 – 3.2 miles

Right now, whenever I go for a run, I just want to keep going. Even if I'm hating the run, I have this desire to keep moving forward. Three miles doesn't do much for me any longer, it feels weak. Cheap. I feel I'm better than that.

Today I had to fight the temptation and the desire to push further. I'm doing well, but I am fearful of sustaining an injury from overuse. I'm nearly halfway through September, and for the most part, I have been injury free. Yes, my back has acted up and threatened to shut me down, but I don't consider the occasional back pain, which I've dealt with my entire adult life, a running injury. Overall, my legs and feet have not been negatively affected from all this running.

I have to balance my desire to run long distances with the risk of doing something that would lead to an injury. I have come too far. Getting injured now would be a disaster.

Tuesday, September 13, 2022
   Day 256 – 4.4 miles

I ran hard today. I felt I had a little "kick" in my legs. I covered the miles on a somewhat hilly course and ran the whole thing in under nine-minute-mile pace.

I still wake up thinking I should go to work. I have many dreams about the school, the teachers, and the kids. In the dreams, I am still the principal.

Wednesday, September 14, 2022
 Day 257 – 7.4 miles

I pushed the distance a little today as a way to build some endurance without doing an especially long run. I felt strong throughout,
but after a slower sixth mile (9:35 pace), I resolved to run faster and
did the last mile in 8:32. I'm not fast like I used to be, but, hey, I'm
54-years-old.

It's been a long time since I have been on the treadmill. The weather
has been perfect for weeks now. It hasn't been hot. It never rains.

Since I don't listen to music when I run outside, the only motivation
I get on these runs is my own positive self-talk. I am full of confidence right now.

Thursday, September 15, 2022
 Day 258 – 5.1 miles

Halfway through the month, and I'm already at 95 miles for
September. This fact motivated me to run five miles today and reach
100 miles for the month. I didn't run fast because tomorrow is my
long run.

Friday, September 16, 2022
 Day 259 – 2.0 miles + 3.15 miles

Our baseball season ended last night. We lost. I never got into the
game which made for another long and frustrating night. I am glad
the season is over so I can finally rest my arm. I'm tired of having to
do things like brush my teeth left-handed the days after I pitch.

Overall, pitching for two teams, with an arm that hurt for most of
the season, I won eight games and lost only four.
***

My run today was a disaster. I set out, full of confidence, to cover many miles. I'm to the point where a long run has to exceed thirteen miles and should be closer to seventeen or eighteen miles.

My intentions ran smack into the face of reality. My legs had nothing in them. Every step was miserable. My legs hurt. My feet hurt. I had no ability to compartmentalize the pain and understand that the temporary pain would soon give way to good feelings. I made it to 1.85 miles, walked for a moment, pushed through to reach all of two miles, and then I quit.

Sometimes I think I am Superman.

And then there are days like this where I realize I'm just me.

And that's a huge disappointment.

There is no way I can run a marathon in November if I keep having results like today's. This was a complete confidence shattering effort.

Saturday, September 17, 2022
Day 260 – 4.25 miles

Yesterday's two-mile run was my shortest run since I did the midnight runs on July 11 and 12 with my aching back. Since that day, I have averaged over five miles a run. I was doing so well...

And me being me, a few hours after that horrible run, I went out and did a faster 3.15 miles. I couldn't let that bad run define me.

Two ends are in sight. The first is the marathon. That's just about six weeks away. I need to get a few good long runs in over the next month to be ready. Once the big race is over, I can scale back a bit and take it a little easier as I look to complete this year-long journey.

Sunday, September 18, 2022
Day 261 – 17 miles

I went to bed last night knowing that today's run had to be very long. For once, I wasn't frightened. I knew what I had to do. There was no alternative. The reality was the reality. I woke up in a good frame of mind, very confident that I could accomplish my goal. Before running, I soaked in the hot tub to warm and loosen my muscles for the multi-hour journey to come.

I have not listened to music on my runs outside, but for today, I made an exception. I put on Pandora's Classic Rock channel and set out into the great unknown. The music helped, not just because it was fun to listen to, but also because it kept my brain occupied with a game I played in my head related to the music. I worked to remember how many songs from each artist were played. The Beatles won with four songs. There were three songs from Queen, three from AC/DC. I also remembered songs from Billy Joel, the Hollies, Fleetwood Mac, Aerosmith, Kansas, and the Doobie Brothers. All of which helped distract me from the task at hand and made covering 17 miles somewhat enjoyable.

As part of the run, I scaled The Monster which is always a challenge no matter what shape I'm in. As long as I can maintain this level of fitness, I am ready for the marathon.

Before my first marathon, way back in 2002, my longest training run was only 17.5 miles. This seems to be the minimum distance needed to be able to cover the 26.2 mile course. I still want to do a few twenty-milers, but with this run now under my belt, I feel much more confident.

I have developed a bad habit on the long runs which would make a nutritionist upset. I have been stopping at a convenience store at about mile eight and purchasing a can of Pepsi and a package of Hostess Snow Balls. I'm certain there are studies that show that drinking soda and eating sweet pastries are detrimental to one's fitness and are not recommended on a run, but I have been enjoying the small breaks I give myself to consume these. I know Power Gels and Power Bars and Gatorade are all better for me. But they also are not as delicious.

Monday, September 19, 2022
 Day 262 – 5.0 miles

I'm still not used to being retired. I often think about the things I (think I) have to do and then realize that they aren't my responsibilities any longer. I had a dream the other night that I didn't do any observations of my teaching staff. One of the teachers in the dream said, "Paul doesn't care any longer." I woke up feeling remorseful for retiring.

Tuesday, September 20, 2022
 Day 263 – 3.1 miles

I didn't get to my run today until 5:30 p.m. After teaching and running some errands, I actually fell asleep. I am wondering if I'm turning into an old man already!

Wednesday, September 21, 2022
 Day 264 – 10.0 miles + 2.0 miles

I set out early today to do a nice ten-miler. My route today involved a lot of long climbs up some difficult hills, some of which I had never run on before. I covered the distance in only 1:35:16. I felt strong and very confident.

With the goal of reaching fifty miles for the week, full of confidence, I went for a second run later in the day. The second run was a disaster. I hit two miles and immediately slammed, head-first, into the "wall." CRASH. I was done. It happened that quickly.

With no energy, I had to walk home which is never fun nor easy. I figured that I didn't need to bring any money with me on this run so I couldn't purchase a drink or any food—even a candy bar.

As soon as I got in the house, I ate whatever bad foods I could find. I saw a Hershey bar, some graham crackers, and marshmallows. About a week ago we used our Solo stove and made a fire outside with Ethan and enjoyed s'mores. Now I made two, without toasting the marshmallows, and gobbled them up. Then I ate apple sauce. I saw a ginger ale and drank it. I was eating and drinking whatever I could, quickly, to replenish my depleted system.

Not only did I have a bad run, but I ended it all with a terrible stomachache.

Thursday, September 22, 2022
Day 265 – 5.1 miles

Today I bounced back and ran on the treadmill making sure to run each mile faster than the one before it. This was my first run on the TM in weeks. I didn't miss it, but it felt good to be running where I have spent the majority of my training miles.

I'm 100 days from completing my year of running. It seemed so close, but then I considered that I still have to run all of October, November, and December, as well as the rest of this month, and the task seemed much too enormous for me to even be able to consider doing it.

I had to remind myself that I'll accomplish my goal by focusing on it one day at a time.

Friday, September 23, 2022
Day 266 – 8.0 miles

Today I was determined to get outside and accomplish a huge training goal. I knew that with eight miles, I'd reach 50 miles for the week.

Saturday, September 24, 2022
Day 267 – 2.1 miles

Today's run was a tedious TM on the treadmill at 5:00 p.m. I covered two junk miles to get the run in, but it felt cheap, like somehow I was cheating because the big effort wasn't there.

Sunday, September 25, 2022
Day 268 – 10.1 miles

This morning started as another disaster. It was cold and damp outside. My motivation level was low. Nonetheless, I stretched, warmed up, and started to head outside when I saw that my Garmin wasn't charged. Without my Garmin, I'm lost on a long run. I've been making up the routes as I go and as I feel. I'm a slave to knowing my mileage, so I had no choice but to use the treadmill and did a solid 10-miles there. I might now change my strategy this week and opt for a bunch of ten-mile runs, rather than the one longer training run.

I have only 28 more miles to reach 200 for the month. I haven't had a 200-mile month since 2009, thirteen years ago! I feel like I have found the fountain of youth.

Monday, September 26, 2022
Day 269 – 10.0 miles

Back outside, I continued running with no set path in mind to eventually reach ten miles. I tried to avoid big hills as best as I could, but that's not entirely possible around here.

Tuesday, September 27, 2022
Day 270 – 3.1 miles

After two longer days of running, and my weekly early morning walk, I did an easy three miles on the TM and then went off to teach college.

Wednesday, September 28, 2022
Day 271 – 10.0 miles

I continued my week of 10-mile days today with my best ten-miler of the year. I covered the distance in 1:32:04. If I can maintain that pace in the entire marathon, I'll come close to breaking four hours. That would be unbelievable.

I'm now at 195 miles for the month. I can't decide if I should do five more miles today to reach 200 or wait until tomorrow...

Thursday, September 29, 2022
    Day 272 – 5.0 miles

For the first time since 2009, I have reached 200 running miles in a single calendar month.

I ran the first mile in 8:59 which is a great first mile for me. This helped inspire me to step it up just a little. I ran the second mile at 8:53 wondering if I had three more fast miles in me. My third mile then came in at 8:19. I wondered where this speed came from. Was I that excited about reaching 200 miles for the month?

Instead of taking it easy, I wanted to see what I had inside. Mile Four clocked in at 7:58. I couldn't believe it! I don't often break eight-minute-miles when I'm out there. I now had just one more mile to go and wondered if I was strong enough to do one more mile at sub-eight pace.

And I did!

The last mile, and I don't know where this came from, except from pure exuberance and determination, clocked in at 7:21.

I finished the five miles in only 41:32.

Friday, September 30, 2022
    Day 273 – 9.0 miles

Today put the stamp on my ninth month. I've made it 75% of the way there.

I "celebrated" by doing nine tough miles. I ran The Monster, but I also added a piece I hadn't done yet this year, an unforgiving windy and steep hill that I call "The Half-Mile From Hell."

I continue to get stronger and stronger. I am doing things as a runner that I haven't been able to accomplish in decades. For a long time this year, I did not see much progress that came from my daily running, but these last two months have legitimized the work I put in to begin the year.

I am very confident right now that I will run a great marathon.

I also believe that I can finally attain my goal of running every day for a year. It seems so close now...

OCTOBER

*"Only those who risk going too far
can possibly find out how far one can go."*
T. S. Eliot

Saturday, October 1, 2022
Day 274 – 3.25 miles

It is always intimidating seeing a blank running calendar as a new month dawns. September was filled with success—great runs and terrific achievements. I did a fifty-mile week! I ran over 200 miles!

And now, I have to start again.

I went out in some heavy rain, did an easy 3.25 miles, reached fifty miles for the second consecutive week, and called it a day.

Sunday, October 2, 2022
Day 275 – 13.55 miles + 6.5 miles

I had a crazy idea for today. I was going to run 26.2 miles, a full marathon, on the treadmill. I'm about a month from NYC. It seemed a good thing to do. I've completed marathons on the treadmill before, but it's been a long time since I had done that. I reasoned that if I could run a marathon today, I'd be more than ready for the real thing in November.

Sometimes things don't go as planned.

I was at 3.4 miles on the treadmill when, suddenly, the computer on the machine stopped working. It wasn't measuring my time or miles.

Not wanting to lose my momentum, I quickly changed my clothes and went outside into a very windy and cold day. I covered a solid 10.1 miles outside. As I approached my home, I went inside for a quick glass of Pepsi, but I couldn't get motivated again and quit the run. I was glad I was able to reach 13.5 total miles of effort, but I was frustrated because it wasn't nearly what I was after.

A few hours later, I decided to see if the treadmill worked. It did, so I did 6.5 more miles (running negative mile splits throughout) and reached 20 total miles for the day in an unconventional manner.

The computer on the TM has never malfunctioned like that before. As the colder air comes with autumn, if the treadmill breaks, I'll be up the creek.

Monday, October 3, 2022
   Day 276 – 3.6 miles

When I first started running marathons, I ran faster and faster races for years:

2002, New York City Marathon – 4:20:47
2003, New York City Marathon – 4:11:44
2004, Baltimore Marathon – 3:55:51
2005, New Jersey Marathon – 3:51:21
2005, New York City Marathon – 3:50:59
2006, Walt Disney World Marathon – 3:34:34
2006, Chicago Marathon – 3:25:16

At that time, I started to believe that I could get even faster and qualify for the Boston Marathon. (I needed to run 3:15:59 to qualify, but those standards have been made even more difficult in the ensuing years.)

I trained diligently, and with great focus, for the 2007 Marine Corps

Marathon, hoping that I would qualify for Boston on that course. My family traveled to Washington, D.C. to encourage me.

Laurie ran a marathon of her own, of sorts, shuttling three young boys all around the city, on and off the Metro, to see me at various spots in the race. It helped; I was doing great, but somewhere around Mile 18, I fell off pace and knew I couldn't make up the lost time. The goal I had worked so hard to attain would remain out of my grasp...

Alex had been a constant source of encouragement and support in my training. He encouraged me when I was on the TM. He'd ask about my runs. He absolutely believed I could qualify for Boston. He was my biggest fan.

The most touching moment in my personal race history came on that Marine Corps Marathon course. I saw my family at about Mile 20 and said, "I can't do it. I won't qualify for Boston today." Alex looked up at me and tears formed in his eyes. He was crushed.

I finished with a great time, 3:30:36, but it was a far cry from a Boston Qualifier. I'd never run a race that fast again. I'd also never come close to reaching the Boston Marathon time requirements. In my older age, that dream has died. I now run races in the 4:30:00 range. That's still good, but good isn't great—and you need to be great to run Boston.

Some dreams remain just that forever... dreams. I was never quite fast enough over 26.2 miles. I can accept that.

What I won't be able to accept is if I can't complete my year-long running quest. I have come so far this year. I have to make it through to the end.

Tuesday, October 4, 2022
  Day 277 – 4.1 miles

The weather has been horrible, nonstop rain. I did four miles on the TM.

Wednesday, October 5, 2022
   Day 278 – 5.1 miles

It's still raining. I was back on the TM. I am glad it is working fine, but I really want to get outside again.

Thursday, October 6, 2022
   Day 279 – 3.3 miles

When I worked as a principal, the job consumed me. One of my goals in retirement is to spend more time with my parents. Today I walked the two miles to their house to visit them and have a catch with my dad. I got my run in later in the day.

The NYC Marathon is one month from today!

Friday, October 7, 2022
   Day 280 – 20.1 miles

Running, for me, is a solitary sport. The vast majority of my runs are alone. It's been just me and the roads. My only constant companion has been God who I pray to each mile.

The daily runs give me something to look forward to each day (and to sometimes dread). The runs also allow me to have at least one success each day, which I believe is very important.

I have a dear friend, Ed, who came over today to do a long run with me as we gear up for the NYC Marathon. Ed is a few years older than me (he's 59) and he warned me that he's gotten a lot slower since we last ran together, which was a few years ago. The pace mattered little to me as we covered twenty miles together. In our lifetime, Ed and I have run hundreds of miles together. We've covered long training distances and run many races together. There are few people in this world who know me as well as Ed because when people run together as much as we have, we expose our deepest selves. We talk about everything. We also see each other at our best and our worst.

As we started to struggle in the upper miles, we talked a lot about how "slow" we've become. Years ago, we used to aim for certain times in our races. Now we just want to complete the races.

There was a time when we thought it mattered what our race times were, but in actuality our finish times don't matter at all. What matters is simply being part of an event, finding things bigger than ourselves, and working to finish what we started.

What also matters is friendships.

Today's run was one of my favorites this year. I wish Ed I could run together every day.

Saturday, October 8, 2022
Day 281 – 4.1 miles

I came too close to a ridiculous milestone today to let the moment pass. I knew with 3.75 miles today, that I would hit 60 miles for the week. That's just a crazy number for me.

Since Laurie and I would head to the beach house to prepare the house for the fall and winter, I wanted to get my run in early. I covered the miles on the treadmill.

I am stronger, I think, than at any time in my whole life.

***

There are more important things than running. Up in Massachusetts, Alex proposed to Perri today and she (of course) said yes! We are delighted.

Sunday, October 9, 2022
Day 282 – 3.1

I was so strong yesterday. I felt invincible.

Today, I had one of my worst runs of the year. At the beach, where it's flat and should have been easy, I had nothing in me. My legs were heavy. Every step brought pain. I did three miles, but it was a huge struggle. I walked during the "run" on four different occasions.

I cannot understand how I can go from being so great to so terrible from one day to the next. I am also not happy that this is happening as the marathon is approaching.

Monday, October 10, 2022
Day 283 – 4.0 miles

Back home, Laurie and I were awakened by a phone call from my mother-in-law at 1:45 a.m. My father-in-law fell and things don't look good.

The police and ambulance were already on the scene, but Laurie rushed down to their house to assist. She is also concerned about her mother and Mark.

***

My run today was as bad as yesterday. I reached four miles, but I again had to take frequent walking breaks. It is clear that I overdid it last week. I bit off more than I can chew. I am paying the price for my over-exuberance. I thought today would be better, especially because I did an early morning walk which usually loosens up my muscles and helps my running.

Not today.

Tuesday, October 11, 2022
Day 284 – 2.5 miles

My father-in-law has been admitted into the hospital. He will remain for close observation and tests.

***

Ethan turns 24-years-old today.

Ethan's job search has been long and slow. He took the day off from his current position as a physical therapy assistant to head to Lafayette College (where he graduated) to meet with the career services people. Hopefully experts can deliver a birthday present of sorts to Ethan.

***

Just a few days ago, I was on such a high. I was doing so well. And now I have hit a wall. Today was my worst run yet. I did only 2.5 miles and that also included much walking. My legs kill, my energy is zero.

I'm in a situation where I need a break to rest up for the marathon. But if I take a day off, I will blow this attempt to run every day. I figured today would be better. It wasn't.

I won't give in. One of these days I'll bounce back. I have to.

Wednesday, October 12, 2022
    Day 285 – 10.1 miles

I woke up early to attempt a long run on the TM on a more forgiving surface than the roads outside. As I ran, there was pain in my left foot near the ankle that was present almost from the start.

When I most need to, I have a way of putting the pain aside and focusing on the task at hand. That task was getting a quality run back under my best. The days of lethargy were shattering my confidence.

After the run, I walked to and from my parents' where I had a catch with my dad. For the rest of the day, I wore a compression sleeve on my foot and iced my left ankle.

Thursday, October 13, 2022
    Day 286 – 1.0 miles + 5.1 miles + 4.1 miles

I woke up very optimistic. My ankle did not hurt at all. I have been fortunate that I have been pretty much injury free this entire year. I attribute this to being fit and doing good stretches and warm-ups before I run.

Today I set out hoping for a ten miler and stopped short, way short, of the goal. As I started warming up with the jump rope, my left foot again started to hurt. I then got on the TM and stopped after only one mile. The pain returned in full. I put the ankle back in the compression sleeve and planned to give my foot the rest of the day off to be better and stronger tomorrow. I kept trying to convince myself that it was okay to run just one mile for the day.

By 10:45 a.m., I was back on the TM running with the ankle support. I banged out a strong five miles and got off the machine itching to do more. I can't leave well enough alone.

This really isn't normal. The running is consuming me. I always think, "I can do more. I should do more."

I did more.

At 2:30 p.m., I went back on the TM for one more run. This time I did four FAST miles. I never went under 7.0 MPH. It was there that I called it a day. I ended up with ten miles for the day, as unconventionally as I accomplished that total.

I am starting to think that I have lost my mind.

Friday, October 14, 2022
    Day 287 – 7.25 miles

I started out today with the hopes that I was strong enough to get a good longer run in outside. In my first mile, actually within the first few steps, even with the compression sleeve on, my foot started to hurt. I stayed determined and just convinced myself to push through the pain for a few miles hoping it would go away or my foot would numb. I figured three miles would be a fair test of my ability to withstand pain and my endurance. By mile 2.5, or so, my foot stopped hurting and I was able to keep going. I didn't walk once on this run. I ran slowly, but I never walked. It was a big step in the right direction.

Saturday, October 15, 2022
Day 288 – 2.75 miles

I have completed 22 marathons and yet, a little more than three weeks from the start of this year's race, I am filled with doubt and concern. My poor runs this week have left me discouraged. The good day yesterday unfortunately gave me very little encouragement.

Sometimes the biggest opponent we have are our own negative thoughts.

I ran only 2.75 miles on the TM early in the morning. We are heading out to Hershey, Pennsylvania to see Ryan and Tiffany. Tomorrow I'll run with Ryan on the big hills by his home. I'm hoping he can make an adjustment on my foot that helps the pain go away for good.

Sunday, October 16, 2022
Day 289 – 3.40 miles

Ryan made the pain disappear which allowed him to take me on a challenging run up what he calls his "monster." I think the hill we ran (maybe it's a mountain) is steeper than the one at home, but it's a shorter trek to the top. It was tough, but when we reached the top, we realized it was only .60 of a mile from his house. It felt like two miles. After slaying that dragon, we took a longer route back to his home.

Monday, October 17, 2022
Day 290 – 10.1 miles

The marathon is now less than three weeks away. With weather being terrible (cold and rainy), I did a strong ten miles on the tread-mill. I am looking to have a bunch of ten-mile runs this week. I don't want to run too far at any one time, but I want to have a bunch of quality longer-type runs of around ten miles. This was hopefully the first of them.

Tuesday, October 18, 2022
Day 291 – 10.1 miles

Another ten-miler. It was again damp and cold outside, so I banged it out on the TM.

Last week I was losing my confidence, this week it's coming back!

Wednesday, October 19, 2022
Day 292 – 13.1 miles

I got a later start today because I spent the morning with my moth-er-in-law helping her with a doctor's appointment. Once I got home, I laced up my running shoes and ran my best 13.1 miles this year. I did the whole thing in 2:03:40 which included one of the bigger hills in my area.

I looked back at the total miles I have run in all of my 16-week train-ing periods prior to my previous marathons. I have a shot to log more miles in training for this race than I ever have before.

I always believe in eclipsing barriers and never placing limits on myself. With my confidence coming back, I feel as strong today as I did fifteen years ago. What a difference a few days makes and pri-marily because Ryan adjusted something misaligned in my foot.

Thursday, October 20, 2022
Day 293 – 3.15 miles

Today I had one of my greatest days in recent memory. I returned to my school and spent the day with everyone. Thomas Wolfe once said, "You can't go home again." He was wrong.

I was a little nervous going back. I did not know what to expect. The answers came quickly as soon as I arrived. The adults and the kids were so excited and happy to see me. There were cheers and hugs. The positive feelings abounded all day long. I thought I might only stay the morning. I remained until 3:30.

After work, I had more good news as Alex came home for the weekend. We did an easy run together. Tomorrow we're going to run much longer. Alex will be running a half marathon on November 6, the same day as my marathon. He wants to do The Monster tomorrow as a training run. I admire that type of determination!

Friday, October 21, 2022
Day 294 – 8.3 miles

Alex demonstrated why he is an impressive runner today. We did The Monster and more.

The Monster is a beast, and it was especially tough for Alex whose runs at home in Cambridge, Massachusetts are mostly flat. As we went up the giant hill, there are a few spots where we could have cut it short. I asked Alex each time if he wanted to take the easier path home. Each time he said, "No." These were tough miles. Alex conquered them all.

Saturday, October 22, 2022
Day 295 – 4.3 miles

Today I did a leisurely jog around home to exceed 50 miles for the week.

And then our lives changed in a major fashion...

After spending the day in New York City with Alex and Perri, we came home to watch the Yankees in a playoff game. Laurie's not a baseball fan so she visited her dad, who is now in rehab, and then her mom. Her mom was not doing well herself, so Laurie made the critical decision to bring her to the hospital where she was admitted.

I went over to get my brother-in-law Mark who will now be living with us for a while. Mark has never lived anywhere without his parents and he was confused, but we made it fun for him. I told him that living with us will be like being on a great vacation.

We knew the day would one day come when Laurie and I would be Mark's caregivers. That day may have just arrived.

Sunday, October 23, 2022
Day 296 – 5.5 miles

If one were to ask Mark who his best friend is, he would tell them that it's me. And I would tell that same person that Mark is my best friend. Laurie and I have been preparing for the eventuality that Mark would live in our home. That this came now is, in many regards, not a surprise. Mark is also not a burden. It's just that life will be vastly different for a while—or possibly forever.

I thought my retirement would give me, for the first time in my life, plenty of quiet time to write, read, run, and possibly even relax (although I do not really know how to relax).

God, though, works in mysterious ways. He often has other plans. I don't tend to question things or ask why certain things happen. They just do. This is now our time to care for Mark, and in a very real sense since I am the one who is home, my time to care for him. If I wasn't retired, Mark would have nowhere to go. With my in-laws in need of serious of medical care, I am the only person who can watch Mark during the day. There is no one else. Laurie and I are his only family.

Our worlds have changed, but I also know that whatever comes next, we will all make it work. I will make this an enjoyable experience for

Mark. Me too.

***

I need to take care of Mark, but I still also need to run. Since it is a Sunday, with Ethan home, I broke free for a while. I ran slowly, but that's fine. At this point, I just want to cover the distances.

The marathon is in two weeks.

Monday, October 24, 2022
Day 297 – 6.1 miles + 4.10 miles

I was going to do ten miles on the TM today, but as I ran, even though he's fine, I thought it was a long time for Mark to be alone in the house with no companion. Mark is excellent at doing puzzles, looking at books, watching television, and occupying himself, but I wasn't fine being selfish long enough to reach ten miles. I took a quick break at two miles to check on him and then did four more. Good, not great. Sometimes the circumstances determine what can be accomplished.

Later in the day, after Laurie got home from teaching, I did another fast four miles to reach ten miles for the day. This might be how I have to attack my long runs during the week at this point.

Tuesday, October 25, 2022
Day 298 – 7.1 miles

This morning, I was back on the TM.

To take care of Mark, I cancelled my college class today. I'm not ready to leave him home alone. I am going to get Mark active. We started this by walking around a half-mile circle outside our house. Mark doesn't exercise much so this was more than a small undertaking for him, but he did great. We'll do this together most days. If Mark stays here long enough, he'll be walking with me for miles and miles.

Wednesday, October 26, 2022
    Day 299 – 5.3 miles + 3.25 miles

Frustration. I have a slight knot, which is the best way I can explain it, in my lower right thigh. It doesn't hurt, per se, but it is annoying, and it impacted my running today. I feel discomfort with every step. I've used ice and the Hypervolt, to try to get some relief, but I'm sure the best thing for it is rest.

I can't give in at this point, so I gathered the courage to run a fast five miles on the TM to begin the day. Later, after Laurie, Mark, and I visited my father-in-law at rehab, I ran home from the health care center to add another 3.25 miles to my total.

Earlier Mark and I walked the circle and then also to the library, about a half-mile away. He tells me that he enjoys the walks. Exercise is good for the soul (and the body).

Thursday, October 27, 2022
    Day 300 – 3.0 miles

I felt like a caged animal today. It was a beautiful day and I wanted to get outside and run far, but I'm not comfortable leaving Mark for a long period alone. This is a big change in his life and it is all so new and confusing. With the marathon just over a week away, I felt I really needed to get out there—and I couldn't. I was frustrated, not with Mark, but with life.

I decided that running up and down the street in front of my house was no more boring than running on a treadmill for long periods of time. This allowed me to be outside and to also check on Mark every few minutes. It wasn't a perfect plan (the run was monotonous). But it worked.

My hope is to get in one last long run outside on Saturday. I have only 65 days to go and I will have reached my goal of running all year and put to rest a heavy burden that I have been carrying in my mind for far too long.

Friday, October 28, 2022
    Day 301 – 5.1 miles

I wanted to run early today so I got going a little after 7:00 a.m. which got me back home before Laurie had to leave for work.

Saturday, October 29, 2022
    Day 302 – 10.6 miles

I was so glad to get outside to run today. This was my last long run before the marathon next Sunday. I did a strong (not necessarily fast) 10.6 miles to reach fifty miles for the week.

As I soaked in the hot tub following the run, I started to think of the marathon next week and my finish time. I used to care so much more about things like that when I was younger. I'd think about how fast I might run the marathon. Since I've aged, and probably because I'm no longer setting personal records, I'm just happy to finish. But, of course, I want to be quick. Deep down, I'd love to be fast again.

My fastest marathon finish over the last decade was in 2014 when I ran the Lehigh Valley Marathon and finished in 4:14:37. That was a small race with an overall downhill trajectory (making it a fast course).

My last two marathons, both in New York City were 4:47:47 (2018) and 4:39:32 (2021). I think I can actually break 4:30:00. Considering my age, I'd be pleased with that. But, in the end, as long as I finish, I'll be happy.

Sunday, October 30, 2022
    Day 303 – 3.1 miles

Today I was the minister at church and delivered a sermon on Eric Liddell the protagonist from the movie *Chariots of Fire.* My message titled, "Run in God's Name" was a simple one—God made us all for a purpose. When we live a good life, when we use our talents to help others and better the world around us, we glorify God.

I'll deliver a similar message at the worship tent for the runners before the marathon next week.

Monday, October 31, 2022
Day 304 – 5.1 miles + 4.0 miles

It is Halloween, but it doesn't feel like it. When one is an elementary school principal, Halloween is a big deal. Excitement abounds everywhere. Today, it was just another day.

I began the day with a strong run on the treadmill.

Then, after taking care of some errands with Mark, just as the trick-or-treaters were starting to arrive, I went outside (Ethan had come home) and ran a fast four miles. My mile splits were great:

Mile 1= 9:08
Mile 2 = 8:49
Mile 3 = 8:40
Mile 4 = 8:03.

It is great when I can get outside and fly. It's been great taking care of Mark, but I am tied to the house pretty much until Ethan or Laurie come home. With the days getting shorter, Laurie most often doesn't arrive home in daylight. She works and then goes to assist her parents in the hospital, nursing home, or both. This has not been easy on anyone. Laurie is wiped out. Completely.

Old age can be difficult. I am hoping that my obsession with exercise helps me have a strong and very healthy old age.

NOVEMBER

"All I wanna do is go the distance."
Rocky Balboa

Tuesday, November 1, 2022
　Day 305 – 3.1 miles + 3.0 miles

I was rushing this morning. After my early morning walk, I did a somewhat fast three miles on the TM before getting ready for college. My parents have volunteered to sit with Mark every Tuesday while I teach.

Again, once Ethan came home, I wanted to get outside for a run. Yesterday, I was fast, and everything felt great. Today's run was a slog—my legs were heavy, and I was slow.

Last month I ran 218.2 miles. That was my best month since I did 222.2 miles in March 2008 which is my lifetime mileage high for any month, ever. I did not realize I was that close to setting a Personal Record for miles in a month. If I had known, I would have run four more miles.

People think that once you reach a certain age, that you can't do things as you used to. I'm 54-years-old. I had surgery on my Achilles. And here I am, as strong as I have ever been as a runner. Limits are constrictions we set for ourselves or that others set for us. I don't believe in limits. I believe I can do anything. Impossible is an illusion.

I now have a goal for 2023. In one month, next year, I will eclipse 222.2 miles. I will always go ever forward and find ways to be better than I was before.

Wednesday, November 2, 2022
Day 306 – 6.2 miles + 3.25 miles

Thirty-eight years ago today, I went on my first date with Laurie. We were in the 11th grade in high school. She was cute and I was surprised she even was willing to go out with me. We went to a Nick Nolte movie titled *Teachers*. I always like to celebrate the anniversary of our first date. We've been married 31 years, but that movie date was the day it all started. I gave Laurie 38 roses—one for each year we've been together.

My run today was glorious. I went out early to get outside (rather than on the TM) before Laurie went to work so we wouldn't be leaving Mark alone for very long, if at all. I didn't run hard or fast, I just enjoyed the cool air and the freedom.

As I ran down one street, the sun slowly rose over the houses and trees. It was spectacular and quite beautiful. In that moment, I sincerely felt the presence of God.

In the evening, I did a comfortable three miles on the TM to have another "double day."

Thursday, November 3, 2022
Day 307 – 3.1 miles + 4.0 miles

I will set my all-time record for most miles in any marathon training period either today or tomorrow.

Heading into today, my lifetime records of miles run during marathon training looked like this:

2007 – Marine Corps Marathon – 674.0 total miles
2009 – New York City Marathon – 670.4 total miles
2022 – New York City Marathon – 667.0 total miles
2009 – Run for the Red Marathon (Poconos) – 663.10 total miles
2008 – Run for the Red Marathon (Poconos) – 657.90 total miles
2006 – Chicago Marathon – 642.50 total miles

2008 – Philadelphia Marathon – 642.36 total miles
2010 – Walt Disney World Marathon – 640.0 total miles

Back when I set those lofty mileage totals, I always headed into my marathon training with a long run so I'd be close to marathon shape at the start. It was a great way to prepare. I wasn't able to do that this year, but I have pushed my training these last sixteen weeks as hard as I could.

Not all of those races were ones I ran fast, but my two fastest races are in there—Chicago (3:25:16) and Marine Corps (3:30:36). There is a lesson here. My best results came when I gave training my best efforts.

I should have a great race on Sunday, but, as always, in the days before the big day, I am filled with trepidation and fear. I know I'm ready, but thinking about running 26.2 miles is something that always scares me. It's not like it's a walk in the park.

Maybe that's why I love it… If marathons were easy, everyone would do them.

Today I ran three miles on the TM miles and then headed, with Mark, into the Javits Center in New York City to the Marathon Expo.

I love the Expo, it is a gathering full of anticipation and joy as the runners descend to pick up their race numbers, race shirts, and immerse themselves in the joy of the upcoming big race. I am always inspired by the Expo. It pumps me up for the big day to come.

Mark loved it as well. He said hello to about a million different people who all were kind to him. He feels as if he made a ton of new friends. What could be better than that?

Once Ethan got home, I went out for a run. That was the good part. The bad part was I went out without eating anything. I hadn't had any nourishment since lunch and at about 2.5 miles, I hit the wall. CRASH. Nothing left. I was done. I stopped for a moment and then walked and ran a bit more before stopping by a bench where I sat for a few minutes. Once I gathered myself, I ran the final mile or so home.

This doesn't happen often, but when it does, it's harrowing. When I crash like this, I get all out of sorts. I become uncomfortable in my own body. I feel completely empty. I wonder how I can walk, let alone run. Being completely depleted of all strength and energy is one of the worst feelings. For this to happen two days before the marathon is a confidence crusher.

Friday, November 4, 2022
Day 308 – 3.1 miles

Today I did three slow miles on the treadmill. I have nothing more to prove to myself and need to take it slowly now, today and tomorrow, before the marathon. Runners are encouraged to scale back their training in the weeks before a marathon. This is called the taper. Because I'm running so much this year, this is going to be my taper. It's all good, or, at least I hope it will be.

Saturday, November 5, 2022
Day 309 – 2.8 miles

And that's that.

I ran (and walked) 2.80 miles to finish my marathon training. In total, I ran 680 miles this training period, an average of 42.5 miles a week. I feel great. I feel ready. I believe I am ready. I hope I'm ready…

I cannot wait until tomorrow!!!

Sunday, November 6, 2022
Day 310 – 26.2 miles

Marathon Day!

In my novel, *Scattering the Ashes,* I describe the main character's experiences as he ran the New York City Marathon. I have been told that is the best description of the race that some have read.

Today's experience wasn't fiction. It was real. Like most marathons I have run, it was great and miserable, inspiring, and discouraging. I felt the greatest I have felt in a long time, and the lowest as well. I couldn't help but keep moving forward toward the ever-elusive finish, but, at the same time, there were countless times when I wanted to simply stop, quit the race, and go home. A marathon brings all of those feelings, desires, and emotions out of me, sometimes at separate times, but, at times, simultaneously.

I love the New York City Marathon. It is my favorite race of the year. Moreover, it's my favorite experience of the year. I have written before that in some ways, this marathon has become part of who I am. A significant part of me lives for the New York City Marathon. I cannot escape it. I am drawn to the race annually. On the years I don't run this race, I dread Marathon Day because I feel a true despondency that I am not part of it. That melancholy stays with me all day and even into the subsequent days.

I love the New York City Marathon. I cannot get enough of the race— it's great size, the loud city streets, the skyscrapers and bridges, Brooklyn and Manhattan. Central Park. And more. So much more. It is all wonderful to me.

I always wanted to be a professional baseball player. I often wish, even today, that I was a New York Yankee. When I run the New York City Marathon, in front of millions of spectators, most of whom are cheering, yelling, and giving high fives I imagine that they're all rooting for me.

Before the race starts I help officiate the services at the Interfaith Worship Tent. I always give a sermon and pray with other runners. I love to share the love of God and his blessings with others, especially on this day. When we give love, it always comes back to us. I encourage the runners to pray at the times when they most think they can't keep moving forward. God gives us strength when we ask and trust in him.

The race, for me, started great. I felt strong and able, and through the first half, I was doing fantastically well. Brooklyn was an absolute joy. As I have done in previous races, I wore a Superman shirt. It's a great rush to run past thousands of people yelling, "Go Superman!" to me.

I was just over two hours at the half-way point (2:01:14).

The Queensboro Bridge that crosses the East River and takes the runner past Mile 16 was a challenge. That bridge presents a steep climb. In my younger years I could scale the bridge without needing to walk, but I wasn't able to do that today.

Once in Manhattan, the wall of sound that comes from the crowds creates a sensation like none other. It is absolutely euphoric, and that enthusiasm carried me past the seventeenth mile.

I was well on my way to a fast time—my fastest in many years, but then, my stomach began acting up. Early this morning, well before the race, I left home feeling somewhat queasy in the stomach. I figured those feelings might pass. They didn't.

This year's marathon was one of warmest on record and we were constantly reminded to hydrate. I drank a ton of Gatorade and water on the course. Often times I consumed two cups of Gatorade at each of the water stops, and with a queasy stomach to start, and all of that extra sugary water added, it led to me being in a somewhat compromised state.

I tried to run through the growing

discomfort, but it was concerning and becoming more and more of a potential disaster. At one point I was desperate and looked for bathrooms at gas stations as I reached the upper miles in Manhattan. By this point, I was hot, sweaty, and drenched in sweat and the water I dumped over my head at many of the water stops. As a result, for reasons obvious or not, the porta-potties were not really an option for me. I try to avoid them at all costs in a general sense. During a marathon, in the state I was in, and with how many people use them in less-than-careful ways, I just... couldn't. There was no way I was sitting in one of those. I figured I would find a way to hold on until the finish line. In order to keep myself together on the course, I had to take frequent breaks to walk. This plan worked, but it slowed me down considerably.

My favorite moment of the race came at about Mile 22. I was completely beside myself and craved soda. There was a convenance store in Harlem that was open, so I stopped in, bought a can of Pepsi, and drank it as many runners passed me. By that point, I didn't care—it was more about survival. The Pepsi was my one joy, even if drinking it added to the uncomfortable feelings I was having inside. When one is in the upper miles of a marathon, much of what one does does not make rational sense.

With just about four miles to go, I knew I'd complete the race. I ran/walked or walked/ran the final few miles to get to the finish line.

I always enjoy the feeling of having a person place the finisher's medal over my head. I save all my medals. I am very proud of them. In fact, Laurie has made shadow boxes that hang on our wall that contain many of my finisher's medals. The medal from the NYC Marathon is always quite impressive looking.

I am proud of my effort and the result.

I wasn't as fast as I would have hoped, but I had a legitimate reason. The stomach issues slowed me down considerably. I finished in 4:38:44. I should have been faster. I could have been faster. If only...

My other favorite moments of today were the times Ed and I were together. We rode in on the bus to the start, both of us officiated at the worship service, and Melissa, Ed's wife, drove us home after the race. I finished ahead of Ed, so after the race, once I had a chance to get out of the crowds in Central Park, I was able to find a place to take care of things and feel better. (I snuck into a pizza joint that has a private bathroom and spent some time there alone.)

Ed has now completed 34 marathons. He's always been a person and a runner I look up to. On the ride home we talked, a lot, about how our times don't matter. It really is all about setting out to accomplish something great.

We kept the faith and finished the race. And in the end, that's all that matters.

Monday, November 7, 2022
 Day 311 – 2.25 miles

Ever forward. With the marathon complete, I have one last running goal for this year. The only thing left for me is to maintain the focus, discipline, and good health necessary to once-and-for-all finish my goal of running every single day in a year. I have 54 more days to go.

I woke up today feeling great physically considering that I had completed a marathon the day before. I didn't sleep all that well because I was still full of the good feelings that accompanied me for finishing my 23rd marathon.

The only part of my body that hurt, slightly, when I got out of bed were my quads and one toe on my left foot. All things considered, I felt better today than I ever have the day after a marathon. The heavy training must have made me stronger and better able to recover.

Today's run was one of my most challenging runs of the year. Even though I felt pretty good, my legs were tired and heavy. I headed out with trepidation. I had never run the day after a marathon. My gait was way off. My movements were stiff and unnatural. Still, I trudged forward. I completed about a half mile on an artificial surface ball-field by my house which helped cushion the impact of each step. I don't know why I had never thought to run there before. Sometimes I don't see the most obvious things.

Later in the day, I took Mark to see my father-in-law. He was so glad to see us, and he was thrilled to see, and hold, my marathon medal.

All that glitters isn't necessarily gold. It can be a metal-like bronze colored substitute.

Tuesday, November 8, 2022
Day 312 – 2.0 miles

On my weekly three-mile Tuesday walk with Mike and Colin, my legs felt pretty good. I found the time to run in the evening once Ethan came home. I did not go far. My left quad was tight, and it is silly to push it at this point. Due to the post-marathon stiffness I feel, I'm still not able to move in a normal fashion quite yet.

Ryan and I talked last night about running the Pittsburgh Marathon together in May. We've talked about this for years, but I was unable to make the time to travel to that race while working. This is one of the things that retirement will bring me, I hope—the freedom to live my life. I always wanted to retire while I was young enough to have the opportunity to experience so much of what life can offer.

Wednesday, November 9, 2022
Day 313 – 2.1 miles

Today was one of those days where I just couldn't get my run in early. With a ton of things to do, I got to my run in the evening and did two miles on the treadmill. I did the first mile at 6.0 MPH, the second at 6.1 MPH. This was the first time since the marathon I was running somewhat normally.

Thursday, November 10, 2022
   Day 314 – 3.1 miles

The New Jersey schools are off today and tomorrow so Laurie will be home which will allow me to be free to focus on myself for a few days. Mark has been great. He and I have fun together, but I am tied to the house for the most part.

I went back and looked at my marathon times from recent years. While my time wasn't great on Sunday, relatively speaking, I performed much better than I have in a long time. I always compare my finishing time to the field. Since 2011, I have usually been in the bottom 50 to 60 percent of all finishers—still, basically middle-of-the-pack, but on the slower half of that equation.

This year, I was in the top 45.6 percent of all finishers. That's still middle-of-the-pack, but it's on the faster end.

The warm weather returned this afternoon, and alone, with no responsibilities, I ran outside. Considering I am just a few days removed from the marathon, my 9:37-mile pace for three miles was very good.

Friday, November 11, 2022
   Day 315 – 3.1 miles

It's still unseasonably warm. I went out thinking that I'd have a quality (and totally naturally feeling) run. My legs, though, didn't respond as I wished and the miles I covered were slow.

I'm sort of in a post-marathon malaise. It's refreshing not to have any specific mileage goals, but at the same time, I don't really know what I'm shooting for right now. For sixteen weeks, I was building up to the marathon, but now I have nothing on the horizon except this daily running task.

My recent runs have been aimless, and this has been somewhat depressing. This is normal. After building up to something grand, the days after seem a bit of a let down.

Saturday, November 12, 2022
Day 316 – 3.25 miles

Each day brings something different. Today, my run felt pretty good. As I ran, I thought about some possible running goals for next year (assuming I can attain my goal this year).

I do not plan to run every day next year too. Once I attain this goal, I will have satisfied that need. I also figured out a goal for the rest of this year. I have some personal records I might be able to reach.

One might think that since I'm running every single day that I'd break all my personal records for miles run, but as I look back, I'm not even close to my best years. There was a period, those years I keep referring back to, when I was in my late 30's and early 40's, when I was at my peak as a runner. I didn't run every day back then, but I ran a ton (and I was strong and fast).

As I looked at my best years, I saw that I have the chance to surpass some of those yearly running totals:

1. 2,025 miles (2009, ages 40-41)
2. 1,804 miles (2008, ages 39-40)
3. 1,774 miles (2007, ages 38-39)
4. 1,670 miles (2006, ages 37-38)
5. 1,603 miles (2005, ages 36-37)
6. 1,473.75 miles (2022, ages 53-54)
7. 1,465 miles (2010, ages 41-42)

I could reach my fifth greatest total miles in a year by averaging slightly under three miles each day for the remainder of the year, but since I also like round numbers. 1,700 miles is within reach. It would be a great large round number. I'll now push myself to see what is possible, but I'd have to run a ton more miles to get there. To reach that mark, I'd have to get close to running five miles each day. I'm not sure I have that much more running in me.

As people get older, many tend to do less. We convince ourselves that our age means that we need to slow down. I obviously don't believe that. I'm glad I'm doing more. I might not be the runner I was a decade or more ago, but I'm close in many regards. I still have great tenacity and endurance.

I don't plan to ever let a calendar define me. I sincerely believe that my best days are yet to come.

Sunday, November 13, 2022
    Day 317 – 4.1 miles

I sometimes get lost in creating lists and trying to figure out where or who I am through numbers. I have, in a sense, found a fountain of youth through my legs this year. My yearly mileage totals in the five years previous to this year were less than stellar:

2017 – 519 miles
2018 – 636 miles
2019 – 381 miles
2020 – 410 miles (Achilles surgery in January 2020)
2021 – 1,023 miles
2022 – 1,477+ miles

In those years, as I got older, I started breaking down. There were times in this period where I had little to no motivation. I remember complaining on a number of occasions that I had nothing inside to give, that I couldn't "dig deep" any longer.

Only now, in retrospect, do I realize that what I was doing, running through the pain, was, in fact, digging deep. I couldn't see that at the time. I could only see my discouraging results.

My poor results led to negative thoughts that promoted more poor performances. I became a self-fulfilling prophesy. I convinced myself that my best days were behind me. As a result, they were.

This year I have found an inner-strength that I thought I had lost. Running every day helped me find it. The last many years, I was worn down in many ways, but through this challenge, I have revitalized myself.

I did a strong four miles on the TM today, running like... a runner. I'm fully recovered from the marathon.

Monday, November 14, 2022
Day 318 – 4.0 miles

There is a common perception that exercise tires people out. I believe this is because immediately after a vigorous workout, people are worn out. The more challenging the effort, the more tired they are. But that feeling of exhaustion eventually goes away, and for a period going forward, the healthy person actually has more energy.

More exercise doesn't wear a body out, it reenergizes it. My body had been reenergized this year.

Now I really feel "back." My running form once again feels natural. Today, I ran in the evening once Ethan got home from work.

The weather has turned, and it is cold all of a sudden. Last week we were in the 70's, this week, it's the low 40's. I don't like the cold. And I especially don't like running in the cold, but it's better than being trapped inside on the treadmill right now.

Tuesday, November 15, 2022
Day 319 – 2.1 miles

I did not have as much motivation today and covered only two miles on the treadmill. Short runs still feel a little like cheating, even now.

As I move forward, I have to expect and accept some setbacks. Today I was feeling some of the post-marathon doldrums. I'm learning to better understand that this is all part of a bigger process.

Day-by-day doesn't mean every day will be great. It means that sometimes I have to grind it out. It also means that there is always the opportunity for tomorrow to be a better day.

Wednesday, November 16, 2022
Day 320 – 4.0 miles

A friend asked me, as so many do, "Why did you retire so young?" My reply is often, "There were a million reasons. A million."

For one, I want (and need) to write. I would never have completed the Roy White book on time if I had to also run a school. I have numerous books that are inside of me (including this one) that I need to get out.

I also want to pursue so many other things with my life. I invested so much of myself in being a principal that I didn't make time to pursue my other interests. I need to get to them while I am still young.

With Mark here, and my ability to do what I want limited now, I have taken up playing the piano. Years ago, when my children were young, I took lessons, but my already limited skills have greatly eroded due to years of not playing. I have found some songs that Mark enjoys so we spend a little time each day singing as I try to reteach my fingers where to go on the keyboard.

I am not very handy nor artistic, but I want to build small things out of wood, and I want to learn how to paint. I also want to learn the aspects of old fashioned wet-plate photography. All of these things take time. I've put off those interests for decades.

There was a shooting at the University of Virginia the other day. As the principal, I always felt that everything that happened at the school was my responsibility. Because it was. The weight of that was a lot to carry. After decades, it became a very heavy burden to always carry.

Schools have also changed. For years, I disagreed with a lot of the decisions that were being made in education. I saw how these were negatively impacting schools, the teachers, and the kids. I fought hard against so much, but the daily battles were eating me up.

I wondered if working at the pace I was under, going hard every minute of every day, was setting me on the path to a heart attack. I never got enough sleep. I was tired, a lot, even if people didn't see that because of the energy I seemed to always have.

A reflective leader or person also knows when his best days are behind him. I knew mine were. I wanted to go out being the best I could be and not be mediocre chasing after more years, more money, or a higher pension. That's not me. I wasn't willing to be anything less than my best. In the end, the students, the teachers, the parents, and the community deserved more than I could continue to give. I recognized that fact.

And, of course, in a way, God told me it was time. I needed to be here for Mark. There are a lot of things I wish I could do right now. I miss the freedom I was finally just starting to enjoy. But right now, Mark needs security and a person he can trust. There are only two people that could have filled this role – Laurie and me. This is my time to be here. God had a plan for me. And I believe that the future has many more great things, but for now, I need to be the rock on which Mark depends. When I get frustrated that I'm tied to my house I remind myself of this.

***

Once Ethan got home, even though it's cold and was getting dark, I managed four miles outside.

Thursday, November 17, 2022
   Day 321 – 2.0 miles

Another uninspired two-mile run. I'm in a slump.
Friday, November 18, 2022
   Day 322 – 5.1 miles

Today I changed my approach and went back to an old habit.

Before I retired, I ran early in the morning before work. Since retirement, I have not been so quick to get running. Today I woke up early and started my day the way I used to—by running. I was able to run five strong miles which is my longest and strongest run since the marathon.

Saturday, November 19, 2022
   Day 323 – 4.1 miles

Teachers get paid in ways other than through salary. The following note came to me through LinkedIn:

> *Hi Dr. Semendinger! I had you as a social studies teacher in 1993. I just came across your profile here and couldn't believe it! I had to reach out!!*
>
> *I've been a high school English teacher for most of the last 16 years and you are still one of the best and most favorite teachers I ever had. I wish you could know what it meant to me to have someone like you who listened to my crazy stories and allowed me to be late to my next class while taking time away from your lunch. You were so kind and generous with your time and for someone who was such an outsider and bullied so much in middle school, what a precious gift that was. I appreciate it even more now as a teacher realizing how little time you actually had and knowing you willingly gave it to me is...I have no words.*
>
> *We read Julius Caesar in your class in combination with the language arts class and let me tell you, that set my entire life trajectory. I fell in love with the bard and just kept on reading everything by him. I became a theater major and then an*

English teacher specializing in his work.

I wanted to let you know what an amazing person you truly are.

***

Ethan, who has had no luck landing a sales job, is considering becoming a teacher. I set up some phone calls and interviews with some of my closest friends and former colleagues to meet with him and share their perspectives on the profession. Much of life is the process of finding oneself and I think Ethan may have just found his true calling.

***

Laurie, Mark, and I are heading to the beach house overnight for a change of scenery.

Sunday, November 20, 2022
Day 324 – 3.1 miles

It was freezing at the beach, but I layered up and did three miles outside in the cold. Strangely, I ran each mile at exactly the same pace. Every mile was run at 9:22. I wasn't trying to do that. It just happened.

With this run, I have logged over 1,500 miles this year.

I also always find it strange to run at the beach in the cold. Two weeks ago, the NYC Marathon was unseasonably warm. Today I was bundled in layers at a place where it's usually hot when I run.

Monday, November 21, 2022
Day 325 – 6.1 miles

I continue to think about what my running goals next year should be. Assuming I complete this year's great challenge, I'll need something else to shoot for. If Ryan and I run the Pittsburgh Marathon, along with my annual participation in the NYC Marathon, that would be two big races in one year. The last time I ran two marathons in a year was 2013 when I did the New Jersey Marathon in May and the NYC in November.

I continually wonder how far I can push my body. At times when I think I'm doing too much, I also wonder if I can do even more.

There are a series of races at Walt Disney World held every year in January. They call these the Dopey Challenge. There are four races over four days: a 5k, then a 10K, followed by a Half-Marathon, and then the WDW Marathon. In 2010, I did what they call the Goofy Challenge—that's the half marathon and the full marathon on consecutive days, but I've never completed the Dopey Challenge.

If Laurie retires at the end of this school year, I might just run the Dopey in January 2024.

Tuesday, November 22, 2022
   Day 326 – 3.1 miles + 3.35 miles

I am to the point where I want to accumulate as many miles as I can. I ran twice today. As much of a drag as it has sometimes been to run every single day, there are times when I cannot get enough.

I was concerned at the start of this year that I might stop enjoying running, I am finding that that isn't the case at all. The more I succeed, the more I want to continue succeeding.

Wednesday, November 23, 2022
   Day 327 – 3.1 miles

Today I went to see the outstanding doctor who performed the surgery on my Achilles in 2020. I presented him with a framed photo of me finishing the marathon to put on the wall in his office. Hopefully that photo will inspire other injured runners to get back at it once they heal. It was great to visit with my doctor. He is older than me by about a decade and he still runs. He understands the passion and commitment of a runner which I always appreciated. I think some doctors would have encouraged me to quit running when I had the injury, but he never did. He promised I'd be a marathoner again.

Thursday, November 24, 2022
   Day 328 – 3.5 miles

The most different Thanksgiving in our lives...

I remember the days when I was little, and we'd gather at my Grandma's house and see the extended family. Most of those people have long passed. Then, for most of our lives together, Laurie and I, and the boys, had two Thanksgivings. The first at noon at my parent's house, a full Thanksgiving meal with my extended family, the second at Laurie's parents, another full meal at around 6:00 p.m. with hers.

This year, it was just our family, Ryan and Tiffany, Alex and Perri, Ethan, Laurie, Mark, and me, but before we ate, we went to visit my in-laws at the Christian Health Care Center. We needed to bring them some joy.

After the visit, Ryan and I ran back home. It felt great to be running outside, especially with Ryan.

For our meal, everyone brought food. I made some pizzas. Laurie made a small Turkey. It was a unique approach to the holiday—a pot-luck Thanksgiving.

After dinner, we played games and had fun. It ended up being the most different of Thanksgivings, but we had our whole family together and that's what the holiday is about.

Friday, November 25, 2022
   Day 329 – 4.75 miles

This afternoon, before I could get outside for a run, I received news that one of my former colleagues, an assistant principal at the high school, passed away suddenly. He would have been just fifty-years-old yesterday.

Some people tell me that I retired too young. I don't think so. When was his retirement? If he had retired, would people have said he was too young?

***

As I ran today, I thought a lot about how life passes too quickly. I couldn't get my colleague's passing out of my mind.

As I ran down one street an older man yelled at me. "HEY YOU!" he hollered.

I looked over, and there, with a huge smile, was my dad. He was out for a walk. I ended my run and walked with him for a few miles. In that moment, I needed to talk to my father, and there he was. I told him of my colleague's passing. My dad replied, "You made the right decision by retiring, Paul."

I know I did.

Saturday, November 26, 2022
     Day 330 – 3.2 miles

When people hear that I am retired, they often ask, "What are you doing now?"

I tell them two things—I teach college and I write.

People understand the college teaching part. Many seem impressed. The writing they certainly don't understand. They have no concept of what it is to spend one's days writing.

Like running, I write every single day. And like running, I have not ever gotten to the point where I hate or dislike writing. In fact, the more I write, the more I enjoy it. I believe I am a better writer each day because I spend so much time working on improving my craft.

Each day I work on this book, I write articles about baseball for my Yankees blog and sometimes for other sites, I add motivational passages to my personal web page, and there are always book ideas that I am working on. Like running, writing is a passion of mine. And like running, if I let it, writing can monopolize my days.

***

I ran outside today and exceeded thirty miles for the week. I'm tired. My legs are heavy when I run. As great as this has been, running every day has taken tremendous effort and I'm somewhat exhausted. I wonder if I have another month in me.

Sunday, November 27, 2022
     Day 331 – 4.0 miles

Today was a depressing day. I spent the morning with my sister at our parent's house talking about all of our parent's wishes in their old age. We wanted to make sure we were all on the same page regarding the life decisions regarding mom and dad that are in our (hopefully far-off) futures.

We have discussed all of this before, but never in so much depth. These were important topics to discuss, but it was sobering. I didn't like talking about the steps we'd have to take to put our parents in a nursing home or to arrange for their funerals. Planning for the future, in this regard, is only preparing for the sadness that eventually becomes part of what life is all about.

After the long discussion, I ran home in the rain. The dark skies matched my mood exactly. When I am in a depressed mood, getting rained on as I run feels like an appropriate thing.

Monday, November 28, 2022
   Day 332 – 3.45 miles

As Laurie came home for lunch, I rushed outside to run. I didn't have a lot of time since I wanted to be back before she left to head back to work and not leave Mark alone, so ran with good speed. I'm trying to stay off the treadmill as much as possible.

Tuesday, November 29, 2022
   Day 333 – 4.1 miles

It was very cold outside this morning so I got on the TM before my parents came over to watch Mark so I could teach at the college.

Wednesday, November 30, 2022
   Day 334 – 6.07 miles

Eleven twelfths. With my successful run today, there is only one more month to go.

In order to satiate this burden that I've been carrying for years, I now only need to wake up 31 more mornings consecutively with the determination, the focus, and the willingness to run.

Like I have had to do each day during this journey, I'll have to block out all of the distractions and the very logical desire to simply take it easy that day. I have to push forward knowing that great satisfaction and contentment lies ahead.

One doesn't come this far to quit.

DECEMBER

"I have fought the good fight. I have finished the race.
I have kept the faith."
2 Timothy 4:7

Thursday, December 1, 2022
Day 335 – 3.1 miles

One thing I need to do better for my next marathon is get faster. I neglected speed work this year as I prepared for the marathon. My focus was mostly on miles, not speed. I'd like to see if I can get faster. I wonder if I can break four hours again. I'm never satisfied with "good enough." I believe as the saying goes, "good enough never is." One book that I once asked my teachers to read was *Good To Great*. Early in that text, the author, Jim Collins, makes the point that "good is the enemy of great." I believe that entirely. I always want to be better.

Running everyday has been an attempt, in a very real way, for me to get better, not only as a runner, but also as a person who can set a task, and no matter how difficult, work to attain that goal.

Today I did three miles on the TM, each a little faster. My last mile was at 8:09. That's pretty quick for me right now.

Friday, December 2, 2022
Day 336 – 7.1 miles

Today I did my longest run since the marathon. Sometimes when I run, I run with great doubt wondering if I can reach my distance goal for that day. Today, I was very confident, and I knew that I'd make it. I had no doubt from the start.

This run pretty much guarantees me another 30-mile week. If I can keep banging out 30-mile weeks for the rest of the year, I'll be thrilled. This will set a nice base to begin my runs next year.

Ever forward!

Saturday, December 3, 2022
Day 337 – 3.0 miles

It has been a long and challenging time, but great news came today. My in-laws' health has improved well enough for them to both return home. This means that Mark is also heading home. His "vacation" is now over. I know that he'll miss it here, we had a lot of fun together these last six weeks, but I am sure this will be a relief to him.

For me, I will now see what retirement actually feels like.

***

I did not have much time to run today. To make the effort into a game of sorts, I ran up to an empty rec football/soccer field and ran the "lines." If there was a line on the field, I followed it. I was sort of a human Pac Man.

Sunday, December 4, 2022
Day 338 – 5.15 miles

Today Laurie and I finished getting the house decorated for Christmas, my favorite holiday of the year. Easter, to me, is the most spiritual holiday, but Christmas, is, by far, my favorite. I love buying gifts for my family members. I love Santa Claus. I still believe in Santa. And, to be honest, I love the hope that comes before Christmas with wondering what gifts I'll receive. I love getting presents! In some ways, I don't think I'll ever grow up. Of course, Christmas is when we celebrate Christ's birth and I always make time to remember the important spiritual side of the holiday, but, as I noted, I also love the presents (and the candy as well)!

After decorating, I made time for a nice free and easy run outside. I ran faster than I planned (most miles under nine-minute pace) but I wasn't really pushing too hard. I usually hate the cold and the weather has been in the low 40's, but I'm not minding being outside.

Monday, December 5, 2022
Day 339 – 5.1 miles

Each day on my runs, I am counting down to the end of this journey. I'm ready for this to be over, but I am enjoying my new freedom. I have no one to worry about right now but myself. This allows me to escape the treadmill, at least until it gets too cold. The freedom, something I have been craving for years and years, just the time to do what I wish, has been great.

Tuesday, December 6, 2022
Day 340 – 4.1 miles

I am looking at my mileage totals for the year and wondering how high I can get that total before this year ends. I am approaching 1,600 miles for the year. I wonder if I can get to 1,700. I have already far exceeded "good enough." I feel I am in greatness territory now. I'm surpassing most of my hopes and expectations for the year. I still have a long way to go, and anything can happen, but now that I have made it this far, I want to continually add more and more miles.

I'm thinking that I'd like to end this year-long process with an amazing month.

Wednesday, December 7, 2022
Day 341 – 4.1 miles

I have proven to myself that age is nothing more than a mindset. If we act old, we become old. I never want to slow down. I have shown myself that I should have many more vigorous years ahead of me.

While there are no promises in life, I believe I can help assure that my later years are healthy and productive by investing in my tomorrows by being active today. One doesn't have to run every day, but I believe people need to exercise in some way most days. Walking, riding a bike, doing aerobics, dancing, even yoga, are all great. An active body, I believe, is one that will stay strong. I believe that an inactive body breaks down. I never want to be a person with an old broken-down body due to a lack of fitness when I was younger.

Today I traded the freedom that comes with running outside with the comfort of staying out of the cold and using the treadmill. The four miles went by quickly. Earlier this year I wanted to sleep while I ran. Now it almost seems as though I could do this in my sleep.

Thursday, December 8, 2022
Day 342 – 4.2 miles

I went outside early for an easy run before heading out to spend the day at my old school again. When I last visited, I assured everyone that I'd be back again, but my return was delayed due to the life events these last six weeks.

I didn't run particularly well today. I was slow and sloth like, I couldn't get loose, but I covered the miles and on days like today, that's all that matters.

Every day is a step closer to achieving this goal. It seems so close now!

Friday, December 9, 2022
Day 343 – 5.1 miles

Our minister called. He has Covid. He asked me to write a sermon and run the church service on Sunday. I am always happy to step in and very honored that he asks me to do this.

I pushed a little more today and reached five miles. I have become very accustomed to the day-to-day ebb-and-flow of running daily. Good days follow bad ones. Disappointing runs follow my best efforts. It's the back-and-forth of being a runner. Part of being an athlete is understanding all of this and working to get through the down periods knowing the good that is sure to follow.

Many athletes focus on the struggles that they are going through, and only see the negative and so they may fail. Winners can see the glory that lies ahead even in the midst of the struggle. I have tried to keep that thought in the forefront in my mind throughout this year. There were days, probably far too many, when I struggled, but even when I did, I knew that something better was coming. This year hasn't been like a race where I can run faster (if I am strong enough) to reach the finish line quicker. The days come as they come, I have had to be ready to face them one day at a time. I am proud of myself that I have. But still, I don't want to get too confident. The year isn't over yet.

I can celebrate in January if (WHEN!) I get there.

With three more miles tomorrow, I'll have another 30-mile week.

Saturday, December 10, 2022
    Day 344 – 3.7 miles

After lunch, I went outside and gave a solid effort to exceed thirty miles for the week.

The entire time I thought about the fact that this whole ordeal will be over in three weeks.

Sunday, December 11, 2022
    Day 345 – 5.1 miles

I jumped on the TM to do a very fast five miles before the church service. I did each mile at 7.0 miles-per-hour or faster. My final mile was sub-8 minutes. I hope I never lose this overall level of fitness.

I greatly enjoy writing and delivering sermons, and I especially enjoy having the authority to oversee and be in control of the entire church service. My mother always said I'd be a minister. That is certainly not in my immediate future, but if I can use the talents I have to bring people to church, and to provide a quality service and meaningful sermon, I'm doing God's work in a good way.

Monday, December 12, 2022
Day 346 – 6.0 miles

I woke up today to a winter wonderland. It snowed last night, maybe only about three-quarters of an inch, but it left everywhere sparking and glistening.

Once the sun came out, I went out into the cold and ran a wonderful six miles. I do not often live in the moment. My mind is always racing and thinking of a million things, but today, for one of the rare times in my life, I decided to enjoy the run and take in everything around me. I saw a more beautiful world than I take notice of most every other day.

As I ran, as I always do, I made time each mile to pray. I thanked God for all of the wonderful things in my life. On days like this, when trees sparkle and glisten and the sun shines brightly above, I feel closer to Him.

Tuesday, December 13, 2022
Day 347 – 5.1 miles

It was back to the treadmill to get my miles in before my final college class this semester. I have enjoyed teaching this class. It kept me connected, in a way at least, to the profession I retired from. I am still impacting, on a much smaller scale, the future.

I just did some calculations and realized that I have now exceeded 1,600 total running miles for the year. I am going to try to get to 1,700. With some good luck, and great focus, I can get there.

Wednesday, December 14, 2022
Day 348 – 5.25 miles

I again went outside into the cold to run. The five miles I covered felt good.

Right now, five miles seems to be about the best I can do. I am having a difficult time finding the motivation and determination to run much further than that.

Ryan told me that he just ran a super-fast 10-miler. For me, right now, ten miles seems impossible. This is one of the mysteries of the sport. Last month I ran a marathon, currently I feel that I am maxing out on these shorter runs. Part of this, I am certain, is that I do not have a race to prepare for. Without the sense of urgency that a marathon brings, I can't conceptualize putting forth the effort needed to accomplish longer runs. Many runners have shared that same experience with me. We often run best when we have a race we are preparing for. It gives our runs a little more of a purpose. Personal goals, such as reaching a certain pace or distance, can also serve those ends, but maybe because a race is public, there is often more of an urgency to train harder, better, or more seriously when one is on the horizon.

Thursday, December 15, 2022
Day 349 – 5.10

In many ways, today feels like my first day of retirement. My college class is over. I will not be teaching next semester (but I do have a class next fall). For a long period, for longer than anytime in my entire adult life, I have no responsibilities. Laurie and Ethan are at work and I'm home, alone, in an empty and quiet house.

I have about 81 miles to go to reach 1,700 miles for the year. I'll need to average slightly more than five miles a day for the rest of the year. I will be very proud of myself if I can finish at that rate.

A strong finish would be the icing on this cake!

Friday, December 16, 2022
Day 350 – 3.1 miles

Some days, it's just not there. I couldn't get into the run today. Nothing felt right. I didn't have the necessary effort, will, or desire to push my body beyond three miles. I'll have to make up two miles to stay on pace to reach 1,700.

Saturday, December 17, 2022
Day 351 – 6.1 miles

I ran hard today so that Laurie and I could leave right after my podcasts for an overnighter at the beach. We don't get a lot of alone time and I cherish these opportunities.

I ran six miles in 51:12 which was my fastest 6-miler on the treadmill this year. This ended a 35-mile week.

Sunday, December 18, 2022
Day 352 – 5.0 miles

This morning I knew I had to battle the cold elements at the beach and run. It turned out to be one of my best runs of the year. I felt fast and was fast. I ran free and easy. I knew from the very first steps I took, that today would be a great day.

My plan was to run about three miles. I was surprised with the fact that I was just over nine-minute-mile pace after one mile. I determined to try to hold on to that speed for the next two miles. When I broke nine minutes (8:55) on the second mile, I thought, "Let me do that again."

Mile Three came in slightly faster still at 8:52. Now I was on a mission. I wanted to add a fourth mile going even slightly faster still!

I was surprised when my Garmin signaled that fourth mile was completed at 8:30. With new motivation, I decided to go all-out and run one final mile as fast as I could. My final mile clocked in at 7:38.

All of the hard work I put into running this year has paid off. I am a much stronger runner today than at the start of the year. I feel different, but more, I am different. In reflection, even if I'm struggling at the time, I have found a confidence in myself as an athlete that had been missing for years. I have run over three hundred and fifty days in a row. I always thought I was strong enough to do this, but I never proved it to myself. I'm proving it now.

Sometimes the knowledge we gain about ourselves doesn't come in the moment, it comes only upon reflection. Sometimes we need to set goals that take time to achieve to find out who we really are.

I am not simply happy that I undertook this challenge, I am happy I am completing it.

Monday, December 19, 2022
   Day 353 - 3.1 miles

Back home, and after some very fast runs last week, I determined today to be smart and just take it easy on the treadmill.

I'm so close to the end, that I'm getting very antsy for it to be over, yet, at the same time, I am starting to think I might miss all of this running.

Tuesday, December 20, 2022
   Day 354 – 5.15 miles

1,700 miles remains possible. With eleven days to go, I have a little more than 39 miles that I'll need to run. This is very doable.

Wednesday, December 21, 2022
  Day 355 – 5.1 miles

I still believe in Santa Claus, and today I brought joy to children in the nursery school program at our church by dressing as him and visiting their classrooms. But, as the children smiled, I was in physical and mental distress.

First, after running on the treadmill, and arriving at the church to suit up, I somehow threw out my back again. It almost doesn't seem fair. My back hurts in ways it hadn't even with the tremendous pain I was in at other times earlier this year. The pain is so intense that there are times when I can barely move. The back pain is terrible, but I have a deeper pain that will last longer...

Just before I headed into the classrooms as Santa Claus, I received notice that one of my dear friends, a leader in my former school's entire community, died yesterday. He had been battling a brain tumor, but I was holding out hope that by some miracle he'd get through it.

As part of his Islamic faith, the funeral services were to be held quickly. It was just a few hours after being Santa Claus that I was sitting with hundreds of grief-stricken people in his mosque attending his funeral service. We then went to the gravesite where, as custom dictates, we took turns tossing dirt onto his casket which had been put into his grave.

One of my goals for retirement was to spend much more time with my friend. His illness changed that. I was not ready to say goodbye to one of this world's finest human beings. My heart is completely empty and in a very real way my heart aches even more than my back.

Thursday, December 22, 2022
    Day 356 – 1.1 miles + 3.1 miles

I won't quit. I can't quit.

With a back that is extremely painful, and a broken heart, I needed to be Santa one more time.

There is a magic in believing, and to see that magic and wonder in the eyes of the little children helped me forget the physical and emotional pains I am having.

Before suiting up as a right jolly old elf, I ran one slow mile on the treadmill. It was not easy. That mile might have been the most difficult one I got through this year.

Later in the day, I visited my chiropractor, who did all he could, and, once home, did three more slow miles on the TM. I am trying to keep this last goal of 2022, 1,700 miles for the year, alive, but it's fading fast.

Friday, December 23, 2022
    Day 357 – 4.2 miles

I am pushing hard, but I might have to determine that some goals just aren't worth it. I went outside for what I hoped would be a comfortable, but slow, five miles. I figured that my back would loosen up as I ran, as it sometimes does. But it didn't. In fact, in the damp cold rain, the weather perfectly fitting my mood and outlook on life, my back seized up at mile 3.5. As impossible as it might have been for me to imagine this yesterday, the pain I am feeling now is even worse than before. Each and every movement kills.

I can barely stand right now, but I'll put up with this for eight days to reach my goal of running each day. I am trying to rationalize that it is acceptable for me to finish with a whimper. I might only be able to complete one-mile runs the rest of the way. This seems like a cheap and disappointing ending to what was a successful year.

I will go back to the chiropractor later today.

Saturday, December 24, 2022
Day 358 – 2.1 miles

It turns out that I have some ribs out of place. My chiropractor spent about 30 minutes with me yesterday working to get everything back in alignment, but he couldn't get me back to 100%. Ryan will be home tomorrow to continue the work on me. My chiropractor knows of Ryan's skills – Ryan did some work there during his studies. He knows the gift Ryan has and is confident that over the Christmas holidays that Ryan can manipulate me out of the excruciating pain I'm in. I also love that he did not tell me to quit. He understands that I have to finish this task. I'm not quitting in the last week.

After sitting with the heating pad, Ethan, who knows a lot about the human body's structure said, "If you're going to run, do it now while the area is at least warm and blood is flowing through it." I followed his advice and did a slow two miles.

Sunday, December 25, 2022
Day 359 – 2.0 miles

As I said earlier, Christmas is my favorite holiday of the year. I love joy and smiles and gifts. Everyone will be here. That's the best present of all.

***

I keep vacillating between three competing ideas as I struggle through the daily pain in my back:

- Just get the days in. Finish the job. The miles do not matter.
- Push to reach 1,670 miles to equal my total from 2006. I only have to run 13.75 miles over the final week to get there.
- Reach 1,700 miles because it's a nice round number and I have worked too hard to get that close and fall short. I'd need to run 43.75 miles in this last week to get there. (This seems

close to impossible right now.)

I did start to feel better yesterday. The ribs grabbed a few times, but it was never excruciating. I know that my daily running doesn't help the healing process.

Today, feeling better, I thought I might have three slow miles in me. At Mile 1.5, my back seized up and I slowly finished that second mile. I'm in great pain again.

I'll put on a happy face on today. I can't hide that I'm in pain, but I can hide how bad it feels.

I'm not complaining. I brought this upon myself. A smarter person wouldn't have run these last few days, but that's not me. I have a goal to complete and I'm going to do it.

Pain is temporary, but pride is forever.

Monday, December 26, 2022
Day 360 – 2.1 miles

Oh, how I hate limping to the finish. Each day, I feel a little better, but not good enough to push the pace or the distance.

Ryan has been working on me each day and it's slowly working. Still, I'm frustrated that I'm going slow and short. I did only two miles again today. It's almost embarrassing.

Tuesday, December 27, 2022
Day 361 – 3.0 miles

As I thought about the last week of 2022, as recently as a week ago, I envisioned a host of entries in this running journal chronicling my quest to reach 1,700 miles for the year. It's still mathematically and physically possible, but it seems much too remote. I can't see it happening.

My back still lets me know that something isn't right. Ryan gave me some great adjustments, but the relief has been temporary. I'm making progress, but it's been slow as Ryan and my chiropractor have explained.

I hate being a two-mile-a-day runner because it seems like I am taking the easy way out. With that thought in mind, I pushed it to three slow miles today.

Wednesday, December 28, 2022
   Day 362 – 6.35 miles + 3.1 miles

I go to sleep each night hoping for a pain-free tomorrow. I'm 37 miles short of 1,700 – this ridiculous final goal I have for 2022. With just four days to go, I know that if I run just a little more than nine miles a day for four days to finish out the year, I can still make it. I'm thinking that these wouldn't have to be single nine-mile runs. I could do three three-milers, or a five miler and a four miler. It is crazy that I am even considering this, but I cannot think any other way. This is who I am.

The runs over this last week have been more difficult than any this year. Quitting has not been an option, but it has taken a lot of courage for me to keep going knowing that the end result will be hours of sharp biting pain.

***

Today was the very last day that I could keep my goal of 1,700 miles even remotely alive, so I threw caution to the wind and did six slow miles to start the day. I then visited my chiropractor who encouraged me to keep running. "Finish it out," he said.

I capped out the day with three more miles on the TM to stay on pace.

Thursday, December 29, 2022
   Day 363 – 5.0 miles + 5.4 miles

Ed came by today to run with me. We did five miles in the early morning together. He wanted to assist me in getting to my goal. This is what friends do. It's sometimes easier to run when someone is there encouraging me. Then, a few hours later, at noon, I did 5.4 more miles on my own.

With two days to go, I am only 16.8 miles shy of my final goal. I am confident that I can get there now. I am willing to accept whatever pain I'll be in to reach 1,700 miles, a final goal for the year. I can't come this close and fall short.

This is what a runner does. It is what runners do. We defy the impossible. We do what is necessary. We overcome. We stretch the limits.

I will not be defined by conventional rules or expectations, I will always aim to exceed them.

I could have taken it easy these last few days and it would have been a successful year. But I would always wonder if I could have done just a little more. I can't end the quest in that manner. No way.

Friday, December 30, 2022
Day 364 – 6.1 miles + 3.8 miles

Two more runs under my belt. I was just under ten total miles today. A goal can be a great motivator and reaching 1,700 miles has been just that. It has helped me keep my focus and do what has been necessary these last few days. I am so close now, I can taste it.

I wish it were tomorrow. Part of me wants to run at midnight tonight to finish the task. I'm restless. With 6.9 miles tomorrow, I'll reach 1,700 for the year.

Saturday, December 31, 2022
Day 365 – 3.65 + 3.25

I didn't sleep much last night. I was much too restless. I woke up for good at about 3:15 in the morning and was ready to go. I wanted to get it over with. It was far too early to go on the treadmill and possibly wake Laurie and Ethan, so I found other tasks, such as reading, to occupy my time.

By 6:00 a.m., I could not wait any longer. I started my stretching and was running on the treadmill by 6:30 a.m.

As the computer registered one mile, I quietly celebrated to myself knowing that I had just completed my perfect year of running. I knew though, that I had more to do. I kept going until I reached 3.65 miles, which seemed an appropriate place to finish that run.

Then later, at about 10:30 in the morning, I went outside to finish the job.

I felt that I needed to do the final run outside, in the fresh air, by myself, but also with God. I prayed. I gave thanks. And I basked in the satisfaction that comes from accomplishment.

When my Garmin registered 3.25 miles, knowing I had reached 1,700 miles for the year, I stopped.

My year of running is over.

I did it!

JANUARY, 2023

"The miracle isn't that I finished…
the miracle is that I had the courage to start."
John Bingham

Sunday, January 1, 2023
    Day 366 – 3.0 miles

I decided to head outside for an easy three-mile run…

Monday, January 2, 2023
    Day 367 – 0.0 miles

I made a big decision today. I think it was a very sound decision. I made a smart choice. Sanity prevailed.

I didn't run.

I let the streak end. I could have run, and a big part of me wanted to run, but I didn't. And that, I think, was a good thing.

***

I never intended for my running streak to continue indefinitely. I wasn't setting out to be a person who never misses a day of running ever again. None of that was ever the intention.

The intention was to run every day for a year. And I did.

But the year ended. The task was finished. When we accomplish our goals, it is okay, and in many instances, it is admirable and smart, to say, "I did it" and to stop. Sometimes we don't have to do more. I am a firm believer in the idea that "good enough never is," but at the same time, I also know that not everything can go on forever. I did not want my running streak to go on forever.

Now, this does not mean that I won't run any more. No, I'll run a lot, or at least I hope to. I will run the Pittsburgh Marathon in May with Ryan. And I plan to be running the New York City Marathon again in November.

We always need more goals and more things to set our minds to achieving, but as we get there, and as we succeed, it is quite alright, and it's often good, to pause, if only for a moment and to say,

"I did it."

And I did.

Lessons Learned

For a long time, I had entertained the idea of running every single day for an entire year. In most years, I rationalized that it was a bad idea. I often figured that the task would become burdensome and would get in the way of everything else I was trying to accomplish and needed to do. In some years I thought the idea was just plain stupid. But the idea never left me. It was with me always, especially as one year ended and a new one was about to begin.

A tried to do this a few times, but I never made it very far.

Still, the idea did not go away...

While I wanted to one day try to meet this goal I had for myself, I was also frightened of the monumental task to have to face each day and find and make the time and give the energy to run. The idea of running every single day, without fail, was daunting and scary and enormous.

I didn't want to get all-in, only to fail. The smarter thing, I reasoned, at least most years, was to not even try.

Life is easier when we don't try. When we try, we set ourselves up for failure.

But, when we don't try, we also lose. We lose because we don't find ways to grow. We lose because we don't gain new experiences. And we lose because we don't have the opportunity to learn from our failures.

Now that I have accomplished this goal, I am proud of myself for having the focus, courage, determination, and tenacity to run every single day for an entire year.

Just like when I first became a teacher, and a principal, and when I finished my first novel, and my first non-fiction book, and when I ran my first marathon, and so much more, as I set out to accomplish something, I learned a ton along the way.

I learned that even as a man in his mid-50's, that I can still accomplish difficult physical tasks.

I learned to run in the cold and the heat. I learned to enjoy running in the rain.

I did a lot of miles on my treadmill. I learned to find ways to conquer the boredom that comes with countless hours of running in the same spot day-after-day-after-day.

I learned to do something difficult even when I didn't want to.

I learned that life begins each and every day. And I learned to plan for the next day by being smart about the current day.

I learned to improvise and make do with what I had at the moment. Wherever I was, I had to run. There was no question of that.

I learned that excuses are just reasons for not doing something. There is always a good reason to not do something. In fact, there are hosts of good reasons. I now know, again, that the key is to push past all of the excuses to focus on the task at hand.

But I also learned that this quest was only part of who I am and who I have to be. I still needed to be present for my school, my family, for my friends, for my church, for my baseball teams, and so much more. I had a job to do (well, until I retired) and other tasks and responsibilities to fulfill. I needed to make time for my runs, but I needed, even more, to see be available for everything else that life required of me for good, bad, or otherwise.

I learned to run when my back hurt and when I didn't think I could even move at all. I learned that even when you don't think you can... you often can.

When I run alone, which is most often, I find the time to pray during each mile. I ran 1,700 miles last year. That's a lot of prayers and a lot of talking with God. I learned that when I run alone, I'm not really running alone. I know that God is always with me. I take great comfort in that.

I learned that there might not be a worse feeling in the world than quitting. As the days became weeks and the weeks became months, and as winter turned to spring, and spring became summer, I knew that I had to complete the task. I wouldn't let anything short of an injury or an unexpected life disaster to get in the way of finishing. There would be no tomorrow if I didn't accomplish today. I had to find a way to accomplish every single today.

I didn't love every run. I hated some. I often counted the months and days until the task was over.

I learned that even though I looked forward, almost from the start, to the quest being completed, that now that I've gotten to the end, I am kind of sad. I don't want to start a new running streak, but I miss the old one. Still, I know that each day will bring with it new tasks and new goals and new dreams.

And I'll always wonder what the next day will bring...

365.2 Going the Distance: Songs to Run By

Here, in no particular order, are my top 100 songs I like to listen to when I run (when I do choose to listen to music). If you want to listen along you can find this playlist on Spotify or feel free to create your own and share it with me on Twitter (X).

https://open.spotify.com/playlist/3pE70Whn7MdYYMQKugONi-H?si=09372df31bf44918

1.   Going The Distance - Bill Conti
2.   Gonna Fly Now - Bill Conti
3.   Heart's on Fire - John Cafferty
4.   War/Fanfare from Rocky IV - Vince DiCola
5.   Training Montage - Vince DiCola
6.   Walk - Foo Fighters
7.   Better Things - The Kinks
8.   The Fighter - Gym Class Heroes
9.   Don't Stop Me Now - Queen
10. Running Down A Dream - Tom Petty
11. Counting Stars - One Republic
12. I Won't Back Down - Tom Petty
13. Get Back Up - TobyMac
14. Born to Run - Bruce Springsteen
15. St. Elmo's Fire (Man in Motion) - John Parr
16. Don't You (Forget About Me) - Simple Minds
17. Need You Tonight - INXS
18. My Life - Billy Joel
19. I Lived - OneRepublic
20. Heroes (we could be) – Alesso, Tove Lo
21. Hall of Fame - The Script, will.i.am
22. Flashdance (What A Feeling) - Irene Cara
23. Turn It On Again - Genesis
24. Till I Collapse – Eninem, Nate Dogg
25. You Shook Me All Night Long - AC/DC

26. Don't Stop Believing - Journey
27. Right Here, Right Now - Jesus Jones
28. Right Now - Van Halen
29. Tubthumping - Chumbawamba
30. Can You Feel It 2021 - Jean Roch
31. Everybody Needs Someone To Love - The Blues Brothers
32. The Lord's Prayer - John Berry
33. Empty Sky - Bruce Springsteen
34. Theme From New York, New York - Frank Sinatra
35. Empire State of Mind - Jay Z, Alicia Keys
36. Empire State of Mind (Part II) Broken Down - Alicia Keys
37. Lose Yourself - Eninem
38. We Are The Champions - Queen
39. Son of Man - Phil Collins
40. Learning to Fly - Tom Petty and the Heartbreakers
41. Got To Get You Into My Life - The Beatles
42. If You Could Only See - Tonic
43. Lonely Boy - The Black Keys
44. Hard to Handle - The Black Crowes
45. You Make My Dreams - Hall and Oates
46. Superman (It's Not Easy) - Five for Fighting
47. Summon the Heroes – John Williams
48. Bugler's Dream/Olympic Fanfare – John Williams
49. New York City - They Might Be Giants
50. I Love NYC - Andrew W.K.
51. Roadhouse Blues - The Doors
52. Break On Through - The Doors
53. Light My Fire - The Doors
54. Scenes from an Italian Restaurant - Billy Joel
55. (Just Like) Starting Over - John Lennon
56. Get Back - The Beatles
57. True - Spandau Ballet
58. Another One Bites The Dust - Queen
59. Handle With Care - Traveling Wilburys
60. As The Rush Comes - Motorcycle
61. Chariot - Gavin DeGraw
62. Counting on a Miracle - Bruce Springsteen
63. The Distance - Cake
64. Eye of the Tiger - Survivor

65. I Will Survive - Gloria Gaynor
66. How Bad Do You Want It? - Tim McGraw
67. Kryptonite - 3 Doors Down
68. No Limit - 2 Unlimited
69. Take On Me - A-Ha
70. Under Pressure - Queen with David Bowie
71. My Sweet Lord - George Harrison
72. Wouldn't It Be Nice - Beach Boys
73. On Top of the World - Imagine Dragons
74. Chariots of Fire - Theme (Vangelis)
75. Suite from Forrest Gump – Alan Silvestri
76. We Are The World - USA for Africa
77. Bad Romance - Lady Gaga
78. Superman (March) – John Williams
79. No Easy Way Out - Rober Tepper
80. Pressure - Billy Joel
81. Clocks - Coldplay
82. Speed of Sound - Coldplay
83. Cold As Ice - Foreigner
84. Fight From the Inside - Queen
85. Strike It Up - Black Box
86. Money for Nothing - Dire Straits
87. Rockin' The Paradise - Styx
88. You Shook Me All Night Long - AC/DC
89. I Don't Wanna Stop - ATB
90. Lonesome Day - Bruce Springsteen
91. Mary's Place - Bruce Springsteen
92. Pink Houses - John Mellencamp
93. Hurts So Good - John Mellencamp
94. Celebration - Kool & The Gand
95. Enter Sandman - Metallica
96. Band of Brothers Suite One - Michael Kamen
97. Rock It (Prime Jive) - Queen
98. We Will Rock You - Queen
99. Tom Sawyer - Rush
100. Burning Heart - Survivor